D0581555

Excluding the poor

Edited by
PETER GOLDING

Published by
Child Poverty Action Group
1 Macklin Street, London WC2B 5NH

© Child Poverty Action Group 1986
ISBN 0 903963 97 3

The views expressed in this pamphlet are not necessarily those of the Child Poverty Action Group

Design by Hilary Arnott
Typeset by Nancy White
Printed by Calvert's North Star Press (TU), London

Contents

Notes on contributors

Meghnad Desai is Professor of Economics at the London School of Economics and Political Science. He has written extensively on poverty in the United Kingdom and in the Third World.

Peter Golding is a Research Fellow at the Centre for Mass Communication Research, Leicester University. He is a member of CPAG's national executive committee and Chairperson of its Leicester branch.

Graham Murdock is a Research Fellow at the Centre for Mass Communication Research, Leicester University, and is writing a book on the future of the television industry.

Alan Tomlinson is a Principal Lecturer in the Chelsea School, Faculty of Social and Cultural Studies, Brighton Polytechnic.

Jan Toporowski is an economist who specialises in the analysis of financial institutions. He works in the City.

Peter Townsend is Professor of Social Policy at the University of Bristol, and Chairperson of the Child Poverty Action Group.

Sue Ward is a freelance journalist and writer who specialises in social security and pension issues. She is a member of CPAG's national executive committee.

Stuart Williams is General Secretary of ATD Fourth World (UK) and has been a member of ATD Fourth World's International Voluntariat since 1971.

Foreword

PETER TOWNSEND

The debate about the growing extent of poverty in Britain in the
1980s is stuck in a rut. It is as if old history was being repeated.
Influenced by deeply entrenched class attitudes, meagre interpre-
tations of human needs on the part of economists and other social
scientists, and above all the timid and fundamentally conservative
approaches to social change by the four main political parties, there
is not much sign of advance on the level of discussion that had
been achieved as long ago as the 1930s. Indeed, there are examples
of retrogression. There were some excellent studies before, or
around the beginning of, the 1939 war, into nutrition and health,
by Sir John Boyd Orr, F Le Gros Clark, Richard Titmuss and
others, which remain to be matched in the 1980s. And much of the
public debate at that time, symbolised perhaps best by the stream
of books from the Left Book Club, the organisers of a large number
of local surveys of poverty and mass observation, reflected a thirst
for first-hand information and a readiness to dismantle and recon-
struct major national institutions if they failed to serve social
objectives.

This book makes at least three contributions to lift the level of
debate. First, it questions the all-too-common assumption, even in
the late 1980s, that basic human needs are physical only. It is not
good enough only to recognise the 'subsistence needs of labour'
and the corresponding subsistence needs of families for food,
shelter, household facilities and clothing, or to qualify that recognition only with token gestures towards the need to observe social
customs and responsibilities, as did Lloyd George and Beveridge
and those social scientists and other professional workers who
helped to pave the way for big changes in the social security system
of the welfare state. People are social beings, with complex social
obligations and relationships. Society defines the roles they are
expected to play, the foodstuffs and styles of life that are available
and much else. People need money and other resources, not just to
get enough food to survive and enough shelter, clothing and other
goods to protect themselves from the elements and the environment, but to fulfil what is expected of them at the workplace, in
the home, the family and the community, and as local as well as

national citizens. The implications are truly immense for social policy. The income required to meet need has to be set at a much more generous level. But society's institutions also have to be reorganised to reflect that 'participative' character of need. All this reflects a political and educational challenge of daunting proportions. Many other organisations than the Child Poverty Action Group will have to play a part if there is to be any chance of success.

Second, modern changes in the geography of the market and the distribution of services can 'create' needs where none existed before. A good example is the decline of village and town 'corner' shops in favour of the mega-stores accessible almost only by car. This (together with the abandonment of resale price maintenance) has made much more unequal the variation in living costs. It has also marginalised elderly and disabled people and made them more dependent than they would be if the distribution of goods and services was organised differently. Similar effects have been created by the pruning of rail and bus networks, the closure of cottage hospitals and the concentration of leisure facilities, as well as by the privatisation of public services. Just when there are increasing numbers of dependent poor in the population, the government is choosing to privatise public services — with the inevitable effect of making it more expensive for poor families and individuals to live on the incomes they have, reach their nearest available services, and obtain substitute services which are as good.

Third, changing technologies and institutions establish needs of a new kind. The process can be quite subtle. Partly, there is a filtering down process from rich to poor. In the early days of radio and television no one in their right senses would have suggested that the mass of the population 'needed' to have radio and television. But gradually the price dropped and the technology improved and radio and television sets became mass consumer goods and hence symbols of citizenship. But more than that. They became necessary instruments of information, like newspapers before them, and are as much used, if not more used, in education and social discourse than are books. However, new needs do not flow from orderly, and ideal, stages of development. Rarely is invention, the design of prototypes, and mass production and consumption a simple sequence of events. Much depends at each stage upon whether profit-making or non-profit-making principles are uppermost and whether public or social accessibility to the modern infrastructures of consumption, communications and service is being maximised. The current arguments, recorded later in this book, about the non-availability of public telephones in remote and poor areas is a good example. Growing dependence on credit facilities from banks and other financial institutions provides another example. Minorities are beginning to recognise that credit-worthiness represents a kind of passport to today's acquisitive society, the lack of which becomes more and more stigmatising. Much the same is true of the opportunity to gain at least a preliminary familiarity with computers and word processors. Computer innumeracy or illiteracy is rapidly becoming socially undesirable and a means of further stratifying an already divided society. It will become a new way of justifying, and condoning, unemployment, dependence and low income. As new styles of service and communication become established, millions of poor people will not have any opportunity of access to these new social goods. They will feel, and be, deprived as a consequence.

Obviously there are parallels to this process in history. Each generation has to confront new problems. But the scale and speed of present developments can be shown to be exceptional even in this century (partly because of the recent rapid growth of multi-national corporations, financial institutions and agencies). People not only feel they have no part in it. They have no part in it. This fosters acute frustration and a deep alienation from authority. People say their lives have become meaningless because their skills are outdated, their potentialities ignored and their worth depreciated. They are not even second-class, more truly marginal, citizens. To the category of redundant employees has been added — certainly for many continuously unemployed young people, disabled people and late middle-aged and elderly people — a new class of redundant citizens.

Great efforts will have to be made to persuade politicians of all parties, professionals and administrators to understand the accelerating nature of this problem. Patterns of social need in Britain are changing rapidly and more radical action will have to be taken to ensure that services and rights to income in the welfare state are brought up to date to reflect those changes. Morality and self-interest are paradoxically intertwined. There has to be a return nationally to stronger collective values — like the right to employment, or the right to an income which is 'basic' in a sense relevant to the 1980s. Otherwise, standards of public order and respect for persons and property will continue to decline, as *Faith in the City* has so graphically described. The social character of need has to be understood. Ultimately, and now is as good a time as any to recognise the full force of this truth, we are one of another.

Acknowledgements

Many people have contributed to the production of this collection. The intellectual stimulus of Peter Townsend's seminal work was crucial in its conception. My colleagues on CPAG's publications subcommittee have provided consistent support and advice. Hilary Arnott has been her usual efficient self in chaperoning the pamphlet through production. Stewart Lansley was kind enough to read and comment constructively on draft chapters. Finally, I must thank all contributors for their tolerance of many editorial suggestions, not all of which were they foolish enough to accept. The fault for any inaccuracies or misconceptions in what follows thus remains theirs.

Peter Golding
May 1986

Introduction

PETER GOLDING

Poverty is a fact of all our lives: The Child Poverty Action Group has spent twenty-one years charting and challenging the grim statistics which reflect the inadequate incomes, shattered lives and material hardship of millions of adults and children in one of the wealthiest countries in the world. Rarely does this allow for a wider perspective, setting poverty in a total panorama.

Yet poverty is created by the way society treats its least well-favoured members. It is inescapably wedded to the degree and consequences of social inequality we are prepared to tolerate or even encourage. Peter Townsend's powerful analysis of poverty in contemporary Britain makes this abundantly clear. 'There are goods, amenities, and services which men and women are impelled to seek and do seek, and which by the tests of both subjective choice and behaviour are therefore social necessities, that have traditionally been excluded from consideration in devising poverty standards.' If people 'lack or are denied resources to obtain access to these conditions of life and so fulfil membership of society, they are in poverty.'[1]

The drift towards a more unequal and divided society has been rapid in recent years. CPAG has made the theme of 'Divided Britain' central to its activities in 1986, and in its budget Memorandum to the Chancellor spelt out in detail some of the indicators of this growing chasm.[2] In particular, CPAG documented the widening gap between the incomes of those in work and those dependent on benefits which have fallen in value as a proportion of average net earnings; between the childless and families coping with the rising costs and diminishing support for those with children; and between the high paid and the millions who earn their poverty at work. Even the usually Panglossian *Social Trends* this year revealed the increasing divide between rich and poor, showing that the bottom 40 per cent of households saw their share of all incomes fall from 10.2 per cent in 1976 to 7 per cent in 1983, while the share of the top 20 per cent had grown from 44.4 per cent to 48 per cent.[3]

But beyond the cold statistics lie the even more grotesque extremes of extravagant inequality, as when Christie's were recently selling a bottle of vintage Chateau Lafitte for £105,000 in the same month that new social security proposals were whittling the incomes of millions for whom even Chateau Sainsbury's is an improbable luxury. These are but the grossest of routine insults which bar large numbers of people from the rights, pleasures, and indeed obligations which garland the lives of their more fortunate compatriots. The following chapters survey that process of exclusion which is at the nub of contemporary poverty.

In the first chapter economist Meghnad Desai examines the evidence for a threshold of income which divides the poor from the remainder. Carefully sorting through the entrails of two of the most important of recent surveys of poverty, he demonstrates conclusively that there is indeed a clear income barrier which draws the line between minimally adequate incomes and those insufficient to sustain a proper and full social existence. Stuart Williams writes from the perspective of ATD Fourth World International, an organisation which works with and for the poorest families, and which has itself laid great stress on the exclusion of these families from the wider society. He adds qualitative depth to the figures provided by Desai, illustrating the corrosive blight which extreme poverty places on the lives of those caught in the margins of our community.

Sue Ward shows how poverty is not just about money but about powerlessness. Taking part actively in politics may be every citizen's right, but it is no more simply a matter of taste and inclination than choosing to have a large roast joint on Sundays. As she perceptively describes, the many expectations and demands which activity of this kind entails put subtle and often unnoticed pressures on those without the resources to meet them. This special case of diminished citizenship is, of course, but one aspect of a larger problem. In so many ways active citizenship requires the capacity to confront the institutions, public and private, which frame peoples' lives. Tackling the town hall, getting to see and challenge your child's teacher, battling with the shop which sold you faulty goods, seeking advice in an unexpected run-in with the law, all demand that easy access to time, telephones, transport, and the soft terrorism of middle-class articulacy which are denied to so many. Poverty excludes, and not least it excludes from power and influence. It is especially timely to bear this in mind in a period in which there is a growing rhetoric abroad which hints, for example in debates about the reform of local government financing, at a price to be put on the franchise.

We are alleged to have moved into an age of leisure, the death of work being a prelude to a new era of free and useful independence. Alan Tomlinson shows how this is true only for those who can afford it. As public leisure provision is curtailed and more and more leisure is dominated by the growth of profitable and expensive private provision, millions find themselves locked out from the new leisure utopia. Jan Toporowski carefully examines the evidence to show how the growth of new financial services by the banks and institutions such as the building societies leaves behind a vast minority population of the unbanked, doubly disadvantaged by their lack of income and by their exclusion from the many advantages of access to financial institutions. For some, the cashless economy means a plethora of credit cards; for others, it means what it says. Money is the poor person's credit card and without it credit is expensive and permanent and frightening debt a common result. Finally, Graham Murdock discusses the exclusion of the poor from the wired society promised by the emergence of new communications and information technologies. He shows that far from bringing a new abundance and variety of information resources, they are actually enhancing the gulf between rich and poor. While the public sector teeters into decay, costly new services fuel the privileges of the information rich. Without urgent action, liberal policies in this area, he suggests, will allow the new communications technologies massively to extend the existing disadvantages of the poor.

Two themes run insistently through these chapters. First, they show clearly how poverty curtails freedom of choice. The freedom to eat as you wish, to go where and when you like, to seek the leisure pursuits or political activities which others expect, all are denied to those without the resources to buy their entry ticket through the many turnstiles our society sets up at the entry points to social activity. To be excluded by poverty is to be denied the full freedom of choice which is supposed to be the pivot of a modern industrial society. Yet millions are so excluded in Britain now.

The second theme is that of participation. As the authors catalogue the demands made by political, economic and social institutions in those who would engage fully in the society around them, it becomes clear that poverty is most comprehensively understood as a condition of partial citizenship. Poverty is not a thing apart, it is a state created by the expectations imposed by an affluent society on those from whom it denies the resources to meet them.

These essays can only be a modest contribution to the urgent task of redefining and remapping poverty in the last decade of twentieth-century Britain. But their lesson is that any adequate approach to tackling the scourge and shame of persistent poverty must embrace very much more than just income support or social security. Poverty is an aspect of all our services and institutions, and poverty policy has to be the kernel of our thinking across a range of issues and initiatives. If we are to end the exclusion of the poor, it is not they but society which must change.

References

1 Peter Townsend, *Poverty in the United Kingdom*, Penguin Books, 1979, p 915.
2 *A Budget to Unite a Divided Britain: Memorandum to the Chancellor of the Exchequer*, CPAG, December 1985.
3 *Social Trends*, **16**, Central Statistical Office, 1986, p 91.

1 Drawing the line: on defining the poverty threshold

MEGHNAD DESAI

For as long as there has been poverty, there have been attempts to question its existence, minimise its incidence or its adverse effects and curb any enthusiasm for its alleviation. People normally of a generous disposition become stingy when it comes to assessing minimum needs. Even advocates of poverty eradication programmes feel forced to be apologetic when accused of including 'frills' on their list of basic needs.

Measuring poverty is an exercise in demarcation. Lines have to be drawn where none may be visible and they have to be made bold. Where one draws the line is itself a battlefield. The process of moving a line a few pounds up or down gets bogged down in prolonged and futile controversy most reminiscent of a rugby game, where the ball moves hardly ten yards in the course of an afternoon.

Those who are suspicious of the notion of poverty insist both on there being a precise and clear definition of what poverty consists of and then on blurring the exercise by pointing to a diversity of needs, circumstances, tastes, propensities, etc. The notion of a poverty threshold, a demarcation line between the poor and the not-poor, is a fraught exercise for just such reasons. A simple threshold figure, easy to grasp and on which to base an anti-poverty policy, would be invaluable, but to be that it also has to be (nearly) universally acceptable. It is in the nature of the social perceptions of poverty in unequal societies that such simple figures are demanded only to be debated.

Any argument in favour of a poverty threshold has, therefore, to be wary of the exercise. The important thing is to make the basis on which the threshold is calculated explicit both in terms of what its constituent items are and why they are there. It should also be open about whose judgment it is that guides the inclusion or exclusion of these items. It has to be debatable and debated by the widest number of people. Only those definitions of poverty which appeal to the widest possible audience will stick.

The political dimension of poverty measurement

A poverty threshold is in many ways a political concept. But while this may always be said, it is the sense in which it is political that is important. The concern with poverty and its alleviation may have originated in the Judaeo-Christian notion of charity (I leave out for the moment other cultures such as the Hindu, the Islamic or the Buddhist). But its conceptualisation has changed with the political environment. The poor law enforcers were local gentry who, as rate-payers and voters, had a stake in the civil society of their times to the exclusion of those they were aiding. As industrial capitalism spread and enfranchisement progressed, the industrial workers (and their families) began to impinge on the politically minded not only because of their actual or potential voting power but also because of the increasing likelihood that the business cycle could deal adversely with them. Thus began the search for a separation of the deserving poor from the shiftless ones. Researchers and reformers like Charles Booth came from within the citadels of the civil society and wished to separate those who should be allowed within the keep and be protected from the incidence of poverty from those who were to be left outside.

The urgency of identifying the poor was made plain by the reverses that the British suffered in the Boer War. Their military vanity hurt, the nation's leaders began to look for possible causes of the deterioration of the nation's stock. The beginnings of the welfare state in the first decade of this century gave a new push to the venture Booth had begun.

The tradition of poverty studies of Joseph Rowntree and many others continued in this shifting perspective. The investigator, with the best of intentions, stood above and outside the world he (as these were almost always men) was surveying. Those he was studying were marginal economically and socially as well as politically. He could decide what the poor wanted or needed, sit in judgment on admissible needs and avoidable frills. The poor were the object of study but had no say in what constituted adequate standards for them.

Full political democracy was long in coming. Universal adult franchise was established in Britain in 1928, but its full effects on the political shape of the nation were felt only in 1945. By then, a 'people's war' had been fought and demands for an implicit contract between the rulers and the ruled about future provision had emerged. The tradition of the expert setting down the menu for universal provision remained. Beveridge relied on previous expert studies and nutritional guidance. But even with him, the distinction between insurance for those in work (the deserving poor) and assistance for those outside work (the indigent ones) remained.

2

This separation of working and non-working poor is fraught with contradictions. In a democratic society, there are no formal barriers placed in access to political rights — of voting, of participation in politics — except the qualification of having reached a minimum age — though, as Sue Ward's chapter shows, informally, low incomes inhibit even political activity. But economically we also live in a capitalist society — a society where allocation of incomes is, by and large, a market process only partially modified by non-commercial considerations. Thus, being in paid work is the predominant way of getting spending power. If normally in work, insurance schemes will provide you with some resources in unemployment or retirement. Work outside the market must be its own reward since no other reward is guaranteed for it. Those not in paid work are not only deprived of normal spending power but also lack the insurance entitlement that unemployed paid workers have. Their claim on resources as citizens is marginal and precarious. Thus supplementary benefit has always been much more stingily given them than unemployment benefit and is quickly withdrawn as soon as there is any hint that the recipient has access to some earned money — by cohabiting, for example.

Thus, political citizen rights have not been fully translated into economic rights. The effect is not abstract. Just as women were the last to get the franchise, they are also left to struggle for economic rights.

Principles for fixing a poverty threshold

A first principle of any discussion of a poverty threshold is, therefore, to start with the individual citizen and her/his rights to an economic entitlement. The entitlement is not a quid pro quo for work done in the past, ie, return of taxes paid, pension contributions made or wages underpaid. Rather, it is a right due to members of the political community to enable them to be full members. There are in every society a variety of non-paid tasks to be done — child-bearing and child-raising, taking care of the household, of the elderly, voting, canvassing at election times, participating in political marches, lobbies, giving blood, helping the disabled. Not all such tasks can be or are paid for on a one to one basis, yet they are essential for the continued functioning (reproduction) of the community as a community. The first principle, therefore, is that *economic entitlement to an adequate living standard should be such that citizens can take full part in the political community*. Not to give this is tantamount to a denial of political rights.

A second principle, however, directly follows from this. If economic entitlement is a passport right, who shall decide on the size of the annual income flowing as a 'dividend' from the entitlement? In the past, it has been the expert opinion, whether individual or a government commission, which has determined the components of the poverty threshold. It is not the intentions (the well-meaningness) of the experts that are in doubt, but it is their *locus standi* in the matter. In a Bismarckian state, with limited popular participation, experts are appointed from above to devise plans to keep the poor docile. In the consensus state that Britain had for much of the twentieth century, the increasing degree of political participation did not affect the supremacy of experts in devising poverty thresholds. The only change was that the poor had perhaps better middlemen (middle-class men, too) to argue their case. But the poor could only assert their voice through agents, not directly. The political community also did not participate directly in the determination of the poverty threshold except through experts. Experts and agents were in *loco parentis* for the citizen.

The consensus state ended with the advent of the Thatcher government, not by accident but by design. Already, in the 1960s and 1970s, the effectiveness of the agents to argue successfully a case for the poor was in doubt since the poverty line continued to be depressed. In many respects, citizen groups learned to rely on direct action, locally or community based, in defence of their hospitals, schools, etc. The women's movement, where a coalition was built on only one common element — gender — taught us that it is possible to organise outside party political lines for a broad spectrum of issues.

It is necessary hence to extend this logic to the poverty debate. If, in defining a poverty threshold, we are looking for a level of living that will enable people to participate in community life, *it is the community which must determine* what the content of such a level will be. Poverty, it is often said, is in the eyes of the beholder, but this is to make it individual-subjective. What is more true is that poverty is determined by the norms and expectations of the community relative to whom certain individuals are poor. So it is social-subjective not individual-subjective. Therefore, our second principle is that *the level of the poverty threshold, ie, the specific contents of the level of living flowing from a citizen's economic entitlement, must be determined by the community.*

With these two principles in mind, the nuts and bolts of fixing the poverty threshold can be tackled. The first principle urges that we sever the connection between paid work and entitlement to a minimum income. It also tells us that the minimum is not related to physical survival — to subsistence — but to being able to perform a whole host of unpaid tasks which the community expects of its citizens and without which it will not function. But once we go away from a need-based poverty line (needs often being defined by experts and not by the needy), the question is how to make the poverty line concrete. It is in this respect that the second principle tells us that it is the community which sets the limits which a poverty line must respect.

The community does this in two ways. First of all, the practice of day-to-day living (the reproduction of daily life) determines empirically what is required in a certain cultural/social context to live as full members of a community. It is the consumption practice — the style of living — that is the bedrock on which any poverty norm must be based. No expert can be trusted to determine this. Experts may be required to take statistically adequate samples to estimate actual consumption practice (eg, the cost of bringing up children in an inner-city environment), but they cannot be allowed to presume what is necessary and what is secondary to daily living. I shall expand below on what it is that the experts must sample; here let me stress that the experts must be subordinate and not superior to the community. They may be independent, they cannot be autonomous; they are servants of the community.

But there is another way in which the community determines the limits of the poverty line. It is the not-poor members of the community who must pay for the poor. There is nothing peculiar to the poor as a group that the community has to make a special dispensation for. While paid work should not be a precondition for income, the sum of all outputs produced for sale (including many public services) forms the pool to be shared out. No community for any appreciable length of time can consume more than it produces, but it can choose to share out what it produces in a variety of ways. Thus, in all societies, the children and the elderly, as well as those who are physically incapable of performing tasks which lead to paid work, are supported by those who produce. Transfer of resources across generations is thus the norm in any society. The way in which such transfers are made — either directly or via the exchange nexus — differs in different societies. The financing of the poor by the not-poor is a case of intra-generation transfer.

The size of the transfer from the not-poor to the poor is an issue over which there will be continuous debate. The feasibility of any poverty line as a guide for policy depends upon whether the community will willingly foot the bill. But, here again, it is easy to exaggerate the peculiarity of the poverty programme. Many public programmes (as well as many private acts) involve transfer from one section to another within the generation of the working population. Thus, adult education in universities, polytechnics and elsewhere is subsidised, as is much basic research. We consider the arts as suitable objects of subsidy. What is much more costly, but not perhaps so transparent, is the transfer to the well-to-do — tax concessions for home-owners, tax deductions for business expenses, subsidies for businesses in various guises such as accelerated depreciation allowances. We also all pay collectively for diseases and accidents caused by the products of tobacco manufacturers, breweries and spirits manufacturers, and automobile manufacturers. There is longer-run damage done by manufactured food products which are injurious to health, by environmental pollution caused by 'wealth-creating' factories, by the noise and fumes of juggernauts whose manufacture is applauded for their greater cost effectiveness.

Living in a world of pervasive transfers, some in good causes and many in dubious ones, the objections that we hear about the difficulty of financing a welfare state or, even more narrowly, a poverty programme can only be political. It is easy to exaggerate the selfishness of individuals and natural to pretend that those who get generously rewarded in the marketplace deserve their rewards, inflated though these may be by tax concessions and hidden subsidies. But the ideology of associating income with prior performance of paid work is so strong that people will ask why should the tax-payer pay for able-bodied men and women, who should be able to help themselves?

It is from this broad perspective that the debate about the poverty threshold must be viewed. Ultimately at issue is who is to define the needs and the resources required for an adequate standard of living — is it the expert, is it the poor themselves or is it the community?

While individual workers such as Rowntree tried to single out the poor and examine their living standards, the practice now is to rely on questionnaires in which the poor as well as the not-poor are surveyed. Peter Townsend's large study of poverty[1] illustrates this transition to the community as a whole as the primary pool of data from which to define the poverty thresholds. But this still leaves the issue of which questions to include in the questionnaire, and who is to frame these questions. There is also the thorny problem of how to relate the responses to these questions to the definition of a poverty threshold.

As we shall see below, in the course of the debate between Peter Townsend and David Piachaud on the definition of a poverty threshold some of these issues were raised and answered. The Townsend-Piachaud debate also informed the next and the latest available poverty study conducted by Joanna Mack and Stewart Lansley on behalf of London Weekend Television (LWT).[2] As I show below, we are closer to the proper determination of a threshold now than at any time previously. It is also helpful that the two studies, although conducted fifteen years apart, reinforce each other in arriving at a similar measure of the threshold.

In what follows, I survey the Townsend-Piachaud controversy

first. Then I look at the LWT study. At the end, the implications of these studies for the nature of contemporary deprivation will be examined.

Townsend-Piachaud debate

Peter Townsend's *Poverty in the United Kingdom: a survey of household resources and standards of living*[3] marks a definite step forward in British discussion on poverty. The book incorporates a definition of poverty as relative deprivation, a spirited argument in defence of this definition and provides results from a questionnaire survey designed to measure relative deprivation. Far from taking the view that poverty is 'in the eyes of the beholder', poverty 'is understood objectively rather than subjectively'. The definition of relative deprivation is then explicit.

> Individuals, families and groups in the population can be said to be in poverty when they lack the resources to obtain the type of diet, participate in the activities and have the living conditions and amenities which are customary, or are at least widely encouraged or approved, in the societies to which they belong. Their resources are so seriously below those commanded by the average individual or family that they are, in effect, excluded from ordinary living patterns, customs and activities.[4]

Armed with this definition, Townsend proceeded to measure relative deprivation from answers to a questionnaire and related this measure to income. He concluded that there was a poverty threshold at 150% of the supplementary benefit (SB) level, below which families were deprived, and that the loss of each pound would increase deprivation sharply. Above that level, extra income reduced deprivation steadily.

This finding was criticised by David Piachaud,[5] who thought the attempt to fix a particular threshold level to be misguided. Piachaud also had several objections to the approach adopted by Townsend. Townsend had computed a deprivation index from answers obtained from the questionnaire and had calculated further an average value of the index for each of twelve income levels and then obtained a measure of 'the break' or the threshold from the relationship between the deprivation index and the income level.

Piachaud found Townsend's deprivation index 'of no practical value whatsoever as an indicator of deprivation'. He argued that for any income level, households showed a great deal of diversity in their score on the deprivation index, this diversity being an indication that the score of any household on the Townsend deprivation index is as much a matter of taste as an indicator of poverty.

There is thus no prior reason why many of the components of the deprivation index should bear any relationship to poverty. Townsend's index offers no solution to the intractable problem of disentangling the effects of differences in tastes from those of differences in poverty.

From these criticisms followed Piachaud's central proposition against Townsend.

The combination of two factors — that there is diversity in styles of living, and that poverty is relative — mean [sic] that you would *not*, in fact, expect to find any threshold between the poor and the rest of society. Townsend's hypothesis that such a threshold would exist is intrinsically implausible.

Piachaud thus poses quite boldly the central issues in the measurement of a poverty threshold. In what sense do Townsend's questions capture the notion of poverty? Is an answer to one of his questions purporting to measure deprivation a reflection of the investigator's tastes, of the respondent's tastes or of genuine poverty? Taking the questions at their worth, Piachaud asked whether, by compressing all his responses into summary measures of deprivation for twelve income classes, Townsend ignored information which may vitiate his conclusion. Was the method of locating a threshold objective or did it prejudge the issue?

The matter, as Piachaud said, 'is, alas, rather technical'. Indeed it is more technical than either Townsend or Piachaud allow for. But the substantive issue is important enough to pursue these technical questions further.

The deprivation index: a measure of tastes or of poverty?

Townsend asked sixty questions of his sample of 2,050 households (6,040 individuals). These questions cover a variety of aspects — diet, clothing, household facilities, housing conditions, conditions at work, health, educational and environmental conditions, etc. The answers in a 'yes'/'no' form were correlated with income of the relevant unit. Now if the answer of 'yes' or 'no' to any question, eg, 'Have you not had a cooked breakfast?', were entirely a matter of taste, one would not expect any correlation between the income level and the answer. The poor as likely as the rich could answer 'yes' or 'no'. The evidence is, however, overwhelmingly against this supposition. As many as forty out of the sixty questions elicited a 'yes'/'no' pattern highly correlated with income. The correlation was significant at 0.001 level, indicating that there was only one in a thousand chance that the true relationship may reveal no correlation between income and the answers to this question, despite the fact that the data showed such a correlation. The lower the income, the more likely it was that a 'yes' answer was found.

Townsend's deprivation index was based on twelve out of these sixty questions, all highly correlated with income. In Table 1, these questions are listed along with the proportion of the sample answering 'yes' (ie, 'deprived') and their correlation with income. They have to be seen not as markers indelibly stamping the respondent as 'poor' if he/she says 'yes', but as evidence that a 'yes' answer is more likely to be associated with a poor family than not. But it is not just the odd individual answer that matters. It is the clustering of several similar answers along with their common pattern of negative correlation with income that is an additional strength of the evidence. Together they improve the odds that a family scoring high (yes=1, no=0) on the index will be poor.

Table 1: *Townsend's deprivation index*

Characteristic	% of population	Correlation coefficient (Pearson) (net disposable household income last year)
1 Has not had a week's holiday away from home in last 12 months	53.6	0.1892
2 *Adults only*. Has not had a relative or friend to the home for a meal or snack in the last 4 weeks	33.4	0.0493
3 *Adults only*. Has not been out in the last 4 weeks to a relative or friend for a meal or snack	45.1	0.0515
4 *Children only* (under 15). Has not had a friend to play or to tea in the last 4 weeks	36.3	0.0643
5 *Children only*. Did not have party on last birthday	56.6	0.0660
6 Has not had an afternoon or evening out for entertainment in the last two weeks	47.0	0.1088
7 Does not have fresh meat (including meals out) as many as four days a week	19.3	0.1821
8 Has gone through one or more days in the past fortnight without a cooked meal	7.0	0.0684
9 Has not had a cooked breakfast most days of the week	67.3	0.0559
10 Household does not have a refrigerator	45.1	0.2419
11 Household does not usually have a Sunday joint (3 in 4 times)	25.9	0.1734
12 Household does not have sole use of four amenities indoors (flush wc; sink or washbasin and cold-water tap; fixed bath or shower; and gas or electric cooker)	21.4	0.1671

Source: Townsend, *Poverty in the United Kingdom*, p.250.
NB: The correlation coefficient measures the strength of the relation between income and the characteristic. The closer to 1 the stronger the relationship, the closer to 0 the weaker.

Thus, for each household, Townsend obtained a deprivation index by adding up the number of 'yes' answers. Two of the twelve questions relate to households where there are children and two are particularly relevant for adults. A household with adults and children could score as high as 12 on the index if it answered 'yes' to all the twelve questions, and for a household without children, the score could be 10. Obviously, therefore, household composition would determine the score as would other characteristics such as income, education, health, wealth, etc.

Townsend looked at the relation between the deprivation index for a household and its net income for each of fourteen different household types — two person households, four person households, single old age person, etc. It was after looking at these different patterns that he proposed a way of combining household type information with income information. This was to compute the SB entitlement for each household and look at its income as a proportion of its SB entitlement. All the households falling within a certain range, say 0-60%/SB level, were put together and their deprivation index was summarised by their *modal* value, ie, the value at which there was the highest number of households within that income range. For twelve income/SB proportions, twelve modal values of deprivation index were obtained. Thus, any one modal value could be summarising the experience of households of different types with different levels of net income but a common value of the proportion of income to SB level. (The modal values as well as the mean values of the deprivation index and the standard deviation of the index within each income/SB range are given in Table 2.)

Townsend then plotted these twelve modal values against the (logarithm of) income/SB level. The graph was 'included tentatively' and the index suffered from 'relative coarseness'.[6] But despite these qualifications, the graph fell conveniently into two lines, one for the five lowest income/SB levels and the other for the seven higher points. From this graph, Townsend concluded: 'As income diminishes from the highest levels, so deprivation steadily increases, but below the 150% of the supplementary benefit standard, deprivation begins to increase significantly. Above and below this point the graph falls into distinct sections.'[7]

Piachaud's criticisms

(a)   Tastes
There are a number of criticisms levelled by Piachaud against Townsend. The first concerns the status of the questions which go to make up the index. Is this a reasonable or an arbitrary set of questions? If a household (in 1968-9, we must remember) answered

Table 2: Townsend's deprivation index: some measures

Net disposable income last year as % of SB scales plus housing cost	y	Score on deprivation index									Total	Number	Mean	Mode	Standard deviation
		0	1	2	3	4	5	6	7	8					
600 or more	7	15	26	23	15	7	4	6	4	0	100	81	2.29	1	1.9226
400-599	5	5	25	35	16	13	4	1	2	0	100	101	2.35	2	1.9462
300-99	3.5	6	21	24	20	16	9	2	1	0	100	337	2.57	2	1.9423
250-99	2.75	7	19	22	22	14	8	5	1	0	100	517	2.62	2.5	2.0988
200-49	2.25	5	15	22	22	19	11	4	2	0	100	874	2.99	2.5	2.1702
180-99	1.90	3	17	18	19	17	15	6	3	2	100	506	3.29	3	1.7765
160-79	1.70	5	17	19	21	16	11	5	4	2	100	567	3.16	3	1.7845
140-59	1.50	1	8	16	18	17	16	12	8	3	100	523	3.94	3	1.8777
120-39	1.30	3	7	18	20	18	11	12	8	3	100	611	3.82	3	1.4098
100-19	1.10	0	3	10	14	19	15	17	12	9	100	420	4.74	4	1.5444
80-99	0.90	0	5	10	11	14	15	16	16	12	100	236	4.93	6.5	1.6479
Under 80	0.70	0	1	11	6	10	12	21	11	26	100	80	5.52	8	1.5099
		4	13	19	19	17	12	8	5	3	100	4,853	3.52		

Source: Townsend, Poverty in the United Kingdom, Table A.11, p.1001. Additional computations done by Dilia Montes of LSE.

'no' to the question 'Have you had a cooked breakfast most days of the week?', should this be taken as a sign of deprivation or just a sign that it did not like cooked breakfasts? Why should the fact that a household 'Has not had an afternoon or evening out for entertainment in the last two weeks' constitute deprivation rather than its habits, which may be stay-at-home? What in effect do the questions purport to measure?

My own response to this last question is that Townsend is trying to measure the community's *consumption practice* or living style. Going out for entertainment, having a Sunday roast, fresh meat with high frequency during a week, inviting friends or relatives for a meal or snack, all such events are what everyday life consisted of in the UK community in the late 1960s. If you consider day-to-day life as marked by these events — meals, going out, holidays, entertaining — then you need to define the typical or normal practice and locate people who, *for one reason or another*, are below the norm. Thus, having fresh meat four times a week would have been the norm and the first job is to find out those who do not have meat that often. The reason for their being below the norm may be either that they don't like meat that much (could be vegetarians) or that they cannot afford it.

Now Townsend did not use any method for separating out those who could afford but did not want from those who could not afford but did want. He relied on the overall negative correlation between the responses and income level as sufficient evidence for concluding (quite rightly) that, on average, given the large sample, it was reasonable to ignore the 'could afford but did not want' category. The correlations for all the twelve questions are quite highly significant and this gives him adequate support. It does not mean that if one took a particular household, you may not find that its high index was a result of peculiar tastes, but it is unlikely to be true in any significant number of cases.

There is, however, one qualification. For three out of the twelve questions, more than half of the sample could be classified as having not had the experience. When trying to capture typical or normal community behaviour, care should be taken to include only those questions for which the majority would be likely to be classified as non-deprived. Thus, even in 1968-9, 67.3% of the population did not have a cooked breakfast most of the week. While the answers were significantly negatively correlated with income, the correlation coefficient is quite low, 0.0559. This means that only a very small proportion (equal to the square of 0.0559 or about 0.004%) of the variation in breakfast habits was explained by income.

One way to get around this problem would be to give different questions different weights in the overall index. Thus, something that was enjoyed by 93% (cooked meat most days) should be given a higher weight (say 0.93) than something enjoyed by only 32.7% (cooked breakfast) which should get a weight of 0.327, ie, equal to the proportion in the community enjoying that experience.

Yet another qualification has to be made about these questions. They should relate to events which are universally enjoyed in the community. If certain groups (eg, old age pensioners) are likely to be precluded for reasons other than lack of income, then the index will distort. Thus single persons, old people and childless households, as well as the household type commonly thought to be typical — married couple with children — should be equally capable of and likely to enjoy the event contained in the question.

(b) *Variability*

The next serious objection Piachaud made has to do with the effect of averaging across all households within a certain range and then using the modal value or the mean as a summary statistic. How serious is this problem? We see that for the upper income ranges, the standard deviation is a much greater proportion of mean score than for the lower income ranges. This variation may be due to family size.

Any process of averaging means that variation around the average is being ignored. Townsend used the modal value, ie, the value recorded by most people within an income group. But there would be households below the modal value and some above. One way to allow for such variability is to compute a summary indicator capturing it. The standard deviation is one such indicator of dispersion around the average value. The larger the standard deviation relative to the mean, the more dispersion there is in the data and the less representative the mean of the underlying information.

In Table 2, the mode and the mean deprivation score as well as the standard deviation are displayed for each of the twelve bands of income characteristics; it is clear that there is much less variation among the scores of the low income families than for the rest. To be able to go without hot meals may be a 'luxury' the rich man can afford to indulge in or not as his taste permits — the poor have less freedom to manoeuvre in such matters. But we must take into account this variation in inquiring about the threshold.

Is there a threshold?

The central issue is about the existence of a threshold level of income, a demarcation level, below which one could say that families are most likely to be poor and above which it is less likely. Piachaud denies the existence of such a threshold and finds many faults with Townsend's procedure. While Townsend's method was quite rough and ready, it turns out that doing regression analysis on Townsend's data confirms his conclusions.

The idea of regression analysis is to check if all the pairs of points on a graph (in this case value of deprivation score and the corresponding income levels) form a pattern, around a straight line or a curve. Could we say that they form a common pattern or two separate patterns? If they form two separate patterns, then we can locate the feature that separates them. They may separate due to the level of income. If so, we can locate the level of income — the threshold — which separates those above and those below in terms of the relation between the deprivation level and income.

A question before we locate separating patterns is to ask what sort of pattern is it? Is the relation between deprivation and income a straight line, indicating a fall in deprivation of so many points for each extra £100? Is it a curve, indicating a faster or a slower change in deprivation as income grows? It turns out that the best overall pattern is a curved line on the graph. Deprivation varies with the reciprocal of income. The lower the income, the higher is its reciprocal and the higher too is deprivation. (Income is defined throughout this discussion as income relative to SB entitlement.[8])

The reciprocal pattern between deprivation and income turns out to be different for the five lowest income levels from that for the seven higher income levels. For the lower levels, it is much steeper, ie, reduction in income increases deprivation sharply. For the higher income levels, extra income registers only a minor drop in what is already a low deprivation level. The two separate patterns explain the data better than a single pattern. There is thus a break in the relation between the mean (average) deprivation score and income and the break occurs at the value Townsend located — above 150% of SB level (details are in the paper mentioned in footnote 8).

There is a further check that we can carry out. The mean score is, after all, a single number to capture the whole distribution and much information is lost. We incorporate, therefore, the variation around the mean within each income level. If the diversity in the scores was due to tastes and not income, then using the mean may overstate the strength of the relationship. So I divided the mean score by the standard deviation within each income level. If the dispersion around the mean was truly random across each income level — ie, if tastes determined whether households scored low or high on the index — then the mean score divided by the standard deviation should be uniform across incomes. The strength of the relationship of the deprivation score with income should be weakened, if not totally obliterated, by this procedure if Piachaud was correct.

The results confirmed the existence of a relationship of deprivation index with income. They also confirmed the existence of a threshold 150% of SB level. Thus the variability in the deprivation scores strengthens the threshold relationship. This is because, as we saw before, the standard deviation falls with income just as the mean rises. The coefficient of variation — the ratio of the standard deviation to the mean — falls with income. There is not much scope for the poor to indulge in diversity of consumption patterns, at least within the context of the questions asked.

Thus, we have reasonably strong evidence that for income above 140-160% of SB level, the relationship between deprivation and income is different from that for incomes at that level and below. The conclusion, then, is that despite the diversity in styles of living and the qualitative flavour of the questions used to compute the deprivation index, Townsend's conjecture about the existence of a threshold level of income, below which deprivation is more severely felt, is confirmed.

The LWT poverty study

The above exercise with Townsend's deprivation score based on twelve questions was originally carried out in September 1981, soon after Piachaud's critique appeared. The Townsend/Piachaud debate, as well as this exercise, influenced to some extent the next large investigation of poverty in the UK — conducted for London Weekend Television.[9] The LWT team commissioned MORI to conduct a survey on poverty. In all, 1,174 people aged 18 and over were interviewed in February 1983. The LWT survey asked questions about thirty-five indicators of styles of living (rather than sixty, as Townsend did), but care was taken to refine the questions to take into account some of the earlier objections. Thus it tried 'to see whether a degree of social consensus exists about what constitutes a minimum standard in Britain today'. The researchers let the respondents, ie, the *community*, decide which of their list of thirty-five items 'are necessary and which all adults/families should be able to afford and which they should not have to do without'. Thus, only necessary items could be included in the deprivation index. A majority of the respondents agreed that twenty-six of the items were necessities (see Table 3); more than two-thirds agreed that seventeen were necessities. Thus, it is possible, not to say desirable, to ask the community to choose which items are necessary and which are not.

Some of the LWT questions cover housing conditions (damp-free home, garden, indoor heating), environment (public transport), furniture as well as food and social activities. It is also striking how, except for the requirement of '3 meals a day for children', it is housing rather than food which ranks high in the community's definition of necessities. The notion of poverty for the community

15

Table 3: *Living standards in Britain* (%)

	Proportion describing items as necessities	Proportion lacking the item	Proportion lacking item as can't afford it
Heating to warm living areas of the home if it is cold	97	6	6
Indoor toilet (not shared with another household)	96	1	1
Damp-free home	96	10	8
Bath (not shared with another household)	94	2	2
Beds for everyone in the household	94	2	1
Public transport for one's needs	88	9	3
A warm water-proof coat	87	10	7
3 meals a day for children*	82	7	4
Self-contained accommodation	79	6	3
2 pairs of all weather shoes	78	15	11
Enough bedrooms for every child over 10 of different sex to have his/her own bedroom*	77	17	10
Refrigerator	77	2	1
Toys for children*	71	5	3
Carpets in living rooms and bedrooms	70	3	2
Celebrations on special occasions such as Christmas	69	6	4
A roast joint or its equivalent once a week	67	12	7
A washing machine	67	9	5
New, not second-hand, clothes	64	13	8
A hobby or leisure activity	64	21	9
2 hot meals a day (for adults)	64	18	4
Meat or fish every other day	63	17	9
Presents for friends or family (once a year)	63	8	5
Holiday away from home for one week a year, not with relatives	63	30	23
Leisure equipment for children, eg, sports equipment or a bicycle*	57	17	13
A garden	55	10	5
A television	51	1	—
A 'best outfit' for special occasions	48	20	13
A telephone	43	17	11
An outing for children once a week*	40	38	25
A dressing gown	38	14	3
Children's friends round for tea/snack once a fortnight*	37	34	15
A night out once a fortnight (for adults)	36	41	18
Friends/family round for a meal once a month	32	32	13
A car	22	37	24
A packet of cigarettes every other day	14	58	6

*For families with children only.
Source: Mack and Lansley, *Poor Britain*

is thus one of relative not absolute deprivation. Rowntree would hardly have considered any of the seventeen items with two-thirds vote as necessities.

The LWT study also distinguishes those things the family did not want from those the family could not afford. This is clearly a tricky distinction and answers may not always reflect true lack of income, since the deprived may learn to live with their deprivation. But at least those who said they cannot afford an item obviously would like it if they could afford it. The LWT team carried out a test of the correlation between 'don't have'/'want to have' response and income for each item and a parallel one for 'don't have'/'don't want' and income. For the first group, thirty-one out of thirty-five items showed a significant negative correlation with income, confirming that it was those with low income who didn't have an item because they could not afford it. For the second group, only eight items were significantly negatively correlated with income, thus showing much greater randomness in the 'taste' for certain items across income.

Thus, the issue of taste in measurement of poverty is dealt with better in the LWT survey. It is neither the standards and preferences of the interviewer nor of the particular respondent which define deprivation. It is the community which chooses which items to rank as necessities and which not. Even when people indicate they do not have an item, care is taken to ask further whether it is lack of resources or lack of desire for the item that is the root cause. But even within the thirty-five items, there are many which only a small proportion of people described as necessities. Avoiding these minority items, the LWT team made an index out of fourteen items, each of which 55% or more of the sample described as necessities (see Table 4).

The LWT data were grouped in twelve income classes similar to the Townsend data. For each level, mean deprivation score and the standard deviation were calculated. Once again, regression analysis indicates that the best pattern was the curvilinear one between deprivation and the reciprocal of income. In experimenting whether there were two separate groups of incomes, three alternatives were tried so as not to prejudge the threshold level. The bottom four and top eight groups, the bottom five and top seven, and the bottom and top six were three groupings tried and a test was carried out as to which separation was the sharpest.

It turned out that the bottom four formed a separate group from the top eight. The mean deprivation score of the bottom four was 2.025 and of the upper eight 0.3626. Thus the bottom four were four and a half times more deprived than the top eight groups. The overall mean was 0.9167. There is no doubt that this separation is statistically valid. Dividing the mean by the standard deviation once again confirmed the results. The break in the LWT data occurs at 133% of SB level for a couple at current rates.

Table 4: *An index of deprivation* (%)

	Proportion describing items as 'necessary'	Proportion lacking these items	Proportion lacking as can't afford them
heating to warm living areas	97	6	6
public transport for one's needs	88	9	3
a warm waterproof coat	87	10	7
3 meals a day for children*	82	7	4
2 pairs of all-weather shoes	78	15	11
toys for children*	71	5	3
celebrations on special occasions like Christmas	69	6	4
roast/joint equivalent once a week	67	12	7
new, not second-hand, clothes	64	13	8
hobby or leisure activity	64	21	9
meat or fish every other day	63	17	9
presents for friends/family once a year	63	8	5
holidays away from home for one week a year	63	30	23
leisure equipment for children (bicycles, etc)*	57	17	13

*relevant for children only
Source: S Weir and S Lansley, 'Towards a popular view of poverty', *New Society*, 25 August 1983

Beyond the threshold: from analysis to policy priorities

A threshold level for poverty has thus been identified from two exercises — one with data for 1968/9 and the other for 1983. Allowing for objections about tastes, about variations within income classes, linear or non-linear relations, we confirm the existence of a threshold. The similarity of the gap between the threshold and the SB level in the two studies is also remarkable. An increase in SB level of between a third and a half is obviously needed — needed in the way need is defined by the citizens of Britain, by the community.

What would it mean to be below the threshold? In Table 4, we have the fourteen items which were in the LWT deprivation index and in the last column we have the percentage of people who could not afford these items. Of course, as the money falls short, different households might do without different items. This would be a matter of taste, of individual household circumstances, etc. But there is a way to the people's priorities from the sample responses. It can be assumed that any household would be extremely unwilling to admit that they go without something because they could not afford it. Thus, the smaller the percentage

18

in the last column, it is more likely that such an item has a high priority. Though not a fail-safe rule, this is a plausible hypothesis.

Looking at the table with this criterion in mind, we see the following hierarchy. The highest priority is toys for children, followed by three meals a day for children and celebrations (4%). The least urgent are holidays (23%), leisure equipment for children (13%) and two pairs of all-weather shoes (11%). Other deprivations are being cold (no heating in home, no warm waterproof coats), eating food you'd rather not (no roast/joint weekly, meat/fish every other day), having old rather than new clothes, etc. These are very basic freedoms being denied to citizens.

But who will provide the extra money? The LWT survey also asked this question. The majority of the sample thought all benefits — pensions, unemployment benefit, child benefit, as well as SB — were too low. What is more, '74 per cent are willing to pay an extra 1p in income tax to enable others to enjoy these necessities'.[10] What more need one say?

Notes and references

1 P Townsend, *Poverty in the United Kingdom: a survey of household resources and standards of living*, Penguin Books, 1979.
2 J Mack and S Lansley, *Poor Britain*, George Allen and Unwin, 1985.
3 As note 1 above.
4 As note 1 above, p 31.
5 D Piachaud, 'Peter Townsend and the Holy Grail', *New Society*, 10 September 1981.
6 As note 1 above, pp 261-2.
7 As note 1 above, p 261.
8 The details of this reciprocal relation are as follows. Full details of this analysis are contained in a paper by the author, 'Is Poverty a Matter of Taste? An econometric comment on the Townsend-Piachaud debate', available on request.

Income : deprivation equations
In each case the first equation is with the mean deprivation score (d) as the dependent variable and in the second equation, it is the mean dividend by the standard deviation (D) which is the dependent variable. R^2 gives the proportion of total variation in the data explained by the equation. The closer to 1 the R^2 is, the better the fit. Numbers in parenthesis are standard errors of the estimates. Roughly the smaller these are relative to the numbers below which they appear, the more confidence do we have in the strength of the relationship.

All twelve observations

$$d = 1.8104 + 2.7562 \, [100/y] \qquad \bar{R}^2 = 0.9609$$
$$ (0.12) \quad\;\; (0.17)$$

$$D = 0.9011 + 1.8028 \, [100/y] \qquad \bar{R}^2 = 0.8212$$
$$ (0.18) \quad\;\; (0.25)$$

Top seven income observations

$$d = 1.9128 + 2.3048 \, [100/y] \qquad \bar{R}^2 = 0.9213$$
$$ (0.11) \quad\;\; (0.27)$$

$$D = 0.7535 + 1.9854 \, [100/y] \qquad \bar{R}^2 = 0.6671$$
$$ (0.21) \quad\;\; (0.55)$$

Bottom five income observations

$$d = 2.4090 + 2.2323 \, [100/y] \qquad \overline{R}^2 = 0.8717$$
$$ (0.43) \quad\;\; (0.42)$$

$$D = 2.0188 + 0.7744 \, [100/y] \qquad \overline{R}^2 = 0.2604$$
$$ (0.51) \quad\;\; (0.50)$$

9   As note 2 above.
10 S Weir and S Lansley, 'Towards a popular view of poverty', *New Society*, 25 August 1983.

2 Exclusion: the hidden face of poverty

STUART WILLIAMS

Why do we need a special explanation for the extreme form of poverty we call exclusion? In Britain, we have a familiarity with poverty and inequality, better documented and researched than anywhere else in the world. We also have a common core of notions and knowledge relating to poverty which is shared by people with often very contradictory political views and which has become an increasingly widespread part of contemporary life. Yet this is not the case where persistent poverty is concerned. It is as though our concern and our debates stop just short of the reality of the population known throughout Europe as the 'Fourth World'. Our campaigns for equality and justice, however determined and committed, do not go quite that far or that deep.

Among the Fourth World, we find all the disadvantages, inequalities and injustices of society compounded among people, families and communities right at the very bottom of the social scale. Their situation is one of serious financial insecurity, appalling housing, lack of basic education and training, isolation from the job market, lack of social and political representation, chronic bad health, the constant worry of having children taken into the care of the local authority, and the humiliation of being dependent on and misunderstood by society as a whole, and by other poor people who are in only a marginally better situation themselves.

Since 1957, the International Movement ATD Fourth World has brought together members of this persistently poor and excluded population, so that they themselves can develop the means to enter the debates on equality, human rights and social justice. In collaboration with other voluntary organisations, government agencies and international bodies, ATD Fourth World runs local, national and trans-national programmes and projects that give members of the Fourth World opportunities to contribute their experiences, knowledge and aspirations towards overcoming the misery they and millions of others throughout the world continue to face.

ATD Fourth World's International Voluntariat, comprising at present 330 full-time trained members, exists to ensure that all the Movement's projects aim to reach the very poorest amongst the poor, and are evaluated with them. It is the Voluntariat's discovery of the unfailing efforts of the very poorest people to build and rebuild their lives as families that is responsible for ATD Fourth World becoming a family movement. This chapter presents these very poorest families' contribution to this discussion of exclusion.

Managing the excluded

Society as a whole finds it difficult to identify the very poorest families. In studies and research programmes on poverty, they appear from time to time but are themselves never the centre of concern when poverty is on the agenda or when anti-poverty projects are set up. When referred to, it is as isolated cases of extreme family misfortune or social maladjustment — 'that one family at the end of the road'; 'that mother who will never cope'; 'those parents who will never learn'; 'that child who always disturbs the class'; 'that lazy father'; 'those mindless adolescents'. If reference is made to these families collectively, it is to these aspects of their behaviour that disturb or shock. For this reason, they do not find sympathy amongst people from other backgrounds. Even collective efforts to represent or defend vulnerable groups in the community — the tenants' or parent-teacher association, the trades unions, the local youth club — draw the line here.

These 'extreme cases', who seem such a burden on society and who appear so indifferent to attempts to help them, are not simply the worst victims of the present recession, or of family tragedy or misfortune. They are the entrenched and persistently poor, whose long history of suffering and struggle has given rise to particular family traditions, social behaviour, work experiences, religious and cultural outlooks and hopes and aspirations. Their lives, and their view of the world, have been forged by the fight generations of the same families have had for their very existence: against the dispossession of their lands, against the humiliations of the workhouses, against being left behind by organised workers, against the unceasing removal of their children, against the dislocation of family life brought about by homelessness and against the ignorance and mistrust of the world at large.

Society manages to ignore this on-going struggle for survival. It appears not to want to accept that sense can only be made of these families' present lives if it is seen in the context of their efforts over generations to survive and integrate themselves into the community. For the families with whom we are in daily contact, this is the most unacceptable face of exclusion. Their lives are reduced to 'a case of this' or a 'problem of that', and society's interaction with them, usually through a professional agency of some kind, bases its intervention on a knowledge of the family that is superficial and case-orientated.

Files held on families in social work or housing offices might go back many years, but these are seen by families who have had access to them as a betrayal of all the positive efforts and hopes that have been so central to their lives. Mary, who had been in nine foster homes in sixteen years, was devastated when she was shown hers. 'I hoped the files would explain my life to me, help me make sense of it all. But over all those years, all they've been doing is put in what went wrong. I don't know whose life that is. It's not mine.'[1]

Society's difficulty in seeing the very poor in the context of years of struggling for security and respect is unjust. The consequences are intolerable. Parents are offered treatment in clinics to develop family bonds that seem to discount the fact that they have been fighting for years to keep the family intact. Barristers representing parents in care proceedings, when faced with a 'do or die' situation, often propose solutions to the court that are actually contrary to the family's long-term interests. Social workers do everything they can to establish visiting arrangements that, unknown to them, overlook the fear of the parents to return to a certain children's home. Through pressure of work, social security visiting officers are regularly forced to interpret a complex family situation without being able to trace files that would help a family justify their claim.

The way the very poorest people express themselves, and appear to lock themselves into impossible situations, clinging determinedly to ways of doing things that seem to contradict what they say, compounds the difficulty they have in making themselves understood and getting their interests represented. A social worker supporting parents in their efforts to send their child to school will see them encourage the child to stay at home. A mother who says she wants her husband to work will be seen to protest if he is helped to find a job.

People's efforts to help can turn against those families they set out to support. And when what is proposed as a solution to the families' difficulties fails, it is most often the family itself who is somehow made to feel responsible. What happens then is that the 'offer' of family support, legal defence, access to children, or a discretionary payment is gradually removed when families do not 'respond' or 'cooperate', do not have the means to take it up, or are not in a strong enough position to query what has been proposed. Even rights to which families or members of a family are legally entitled (legal aid, for example) are withheld when they are unable to take advantage of them.[2] These rights are further weakened when those who apply them, and society as a whole, have the unsettling feeling that such rights cannot really be justified in the majority of cases.

In this way, the poorest families are excluded from being able truly to communicate who they are, what they believe, how they want to live and with whom, what they want to achieve, and how their achievement should be measured. They are excluded because society continues to paint its own image of them, rather than insisting that, individually and collectively, they have the means to make sense of their experiences and represent themselves and their interests.

Exclusion from contributing to society

Out of a sample of 165 adults contacted during 1984 and 1985 through Frimhurst, ATD Fourth World's family centre in Surrey, forty-eight were unable to read a popular newspaper and write more than the simplest of phrases. Out of a group of sixteen extremely disadvantaged young people under 25 living in London whom we brought together to prepare a theatre presentation about their lives for International Youth Year,[3] only one had an 'O' level, only three had a CSE and twelve had no qualifications at all. Only three of the same sixteen were in work in December 1985.

It is difficult, if not impossible, to ascertain present levels of adult literacy and numeracy in the UK, in spite of the enormous investment in literacy programmes nationally and the considerable efforts of schools to ensure that all school-leavers are equipped with these basic skills. Yet the view the poorest people have of the world, and their relationship with it, is drastically affected by the limits to their abilities to read, write and calculate. Bus maps, job application forms, newspapers or the unhelpful plain labels on the 'Basics' range of tinned foods are out of reach. So, too often, are the means for doing something about it.

'When you've always been frightened of school, how can you face it again when you're 22? They all want to know what I'm doing learning to read and write at my age!'

Bill, from Northern Ireland, added: 'Where can people like us go to learn?' As for Mandy: 'I didn't even get offered a YTS place. She could see that I couldn't write my name.' This lack of basic education distorts relationships with the world at large but, even more seriously, also within the family. 'I blame it on not having my glasses when the kids ask me to read them something', said Michael, whose two daughters are in infant school. He is unable to admit to them that he cannot read.

When a delegation of Fourth World young people met with the Under Secretary of State at the Department of Employment in May 1985,[4] they asked him to understand that they are effectively excluded from avenues of learning. Literacy and basic skills teachers who try to help are rarely able to take account of the humiliation and sense of failure they have to overcome, and have not yet found a way to leave the school and go out to those whose irregular attendance in the classroom betrays what can be an intense motivation to learn.

Peter, aged 17, told us about the work-experience scheme organised for him by his school when he was 13. The owner of the farm that offered him a place encouraged him to work there as much as four days a week, which he agreed to. As a result, he was only in school half a day a week for much of his last two years of schooling. At 16, he joined a YTS project. After several months, he changed schemes to be on one which included one hour of reading and writing tuition a week. When he asked if this could be increased, his supervisor was not encouraging: 'Where do you think you are? You're not here to dawdle!' Unwilling to try another government scheme or go alone to local literacy and numeracy classes, and unable to secure work through his local job centre, he has for the past nine months been picking up temporary work with demolition gangs, cleaners and haulage contractors, none of whom wish to invest in his education or training.

Fourth World adults have always found it difficult to secure work that is regular and properly paid. The present levels of unemployment in this country are having a devastating effect on them. The dirtiest, low-status jobs, like cleaning trains, sweeping up in factories, hotel laundry work and kitchen and hospital porterage, are now being taken up by semi-skilled and skilled workers who would not have agreed to do such work in the past.

In the search for new kinds of work, useful leisure, voluntary initiative and community service, they have no skills, competences or colleagues with which to play a role. They are excluded from the respect given by society to workers, and excluded from the admiration accorded to those who 'make the best' of unemployment. What is even worse, they know that should higher levels of employment return, they will be the last to return to work, they will have lost the little know-how they possess, and they will have seen their health and strength dissipated by years of inactivity.

With this future before them, they see their children growing up with no contact with working people, with no experience of being with others, no experience of contributing to some common task or to the well-being of the community.[5] Their children are growing up strangers to the world of work and to the world of comradeship that goes with it.

Exclusion from an independent existence

The poorer a family, the greater is the paradox they experience of being misunderstood, rejected and excluded by everyone, and at the same time having to depend on everyone — neighbours, employers, clerks at the social security office, organisations that give handouts, teachers, caretakers. Money, the secure tenure of a home and work all come from other people and are dependent to a frightening extent on their kindness and humour. Everywhere, the poorest people have to ask for money, for housing, for work and for help. At the housing office or social security department, the poorest people are not prepared for what they are asked, or for what will happen if they answer in a certain way. Yet they go as it is only through these offices that they can try and get what they need.

This sense of dependence is reinforced by the impression given by people who administer local housing policy or the benefits office to the poorest families that they are a burden and 'cost a lot'. Here, perhaps, lies the crux of the problem of dependence for Fourth World families. They are forced to rely for their livelihood on the image that employees in these offices, these representatives of society, have of them. Their lives are subject to other people's understanding of poverty, and morality and even courage. They are dependent on other people's understanding and sense of justice, on other people's interpretation of the facts, and on other people's knowledge of the rights associated with their situation. They are dependent on a society that organises itself to intervene in an individual's or a family's daily life without their invitation or consent, and which generally avoids being held publicly accountable for its actions.

Parents whose children are in care can often do nothing when they discover that their child has been abused by foster parents, or that their teenage daughter has become pregnant in the care of the local authority. There is nothing they are allowed to do to prevent this kind of thing happening, and nothing they can do to ensure that it will not happen again. They are in a position of helplessness.

Even in everyday things like safety in the home, very vulnerable families are equally powerless. Recently, a mother and her three children had no choice but to stand by whilst a social security officer and a shopkeeper who supplies second-hand cookers to families on supplementary benefit discussed the safety of the cooker she had been supplied with. The mother believed it was in a dangerous condition, but was unsuccessful in insisting on its replacement because it had been bought from the shop by the DHSS independently of the mother. When the cooker exploded in the kitchen, the mother's protest to the social security office resulted in a discharge of the responsibility on to her: 'I hope you bothered to get a guarantee!'

Although the regulations relating to the placement of children in care, and to the supply of second-hand domestic appliances, are again being reviewed, what is so devastating about this kind of situation is not just that the persistently poor are forced into a situation of total dependence on people they do not know, and who do not know them, but that as parents and consumers, they are denied recognition of their right to act independently and influence and control what happens to them.[6]

People who are totally dependent on others have to rely on them for financial support. For the vast majority of families known to ATD Fourth World in Britain, social security benefits in the form of supplementary benefit and invalidity pensions provide the major source of income. For individuals and families who are long-term recipients of these benefits, the present levels are quite inadequate to meet essential basic needs. Buying new clothes and shoes, replacing household equipment and furniture, making regular journeys by bus or by train to find work or visit relatives and friends are out of the question.

For the very poorest families, the position is even worse. Families have to live without heating for weeks on end. Some have to cope with the gas, electricity and even the water cut off. Children are forced to share clothes and shoes, even to the point of one having to stay at home so a brother or sister can go out. Mothers are unable to afford bus fares to collect their children from school. Parents and children sell off what is left in the house to stop debt-collectors breaking in. Families have to beg to be able to bury their dead. This is what life is like for the poorest people in Britain today.

For the very poorest families, it is not only a question of the levels of benefits, but also of the role these benefits play in their lives. Supplementary benefit fails to provide a real safety net since its payment is dependent on factors outside the control of the recipients, and because the social security system is not planned to take account of the permanent irregularity and imbalance of the budgets of the poorest people. Advances and loans begged off shopkeepers and friends, food from the social worker or a local charity for the weekend, milk tokens sold to a neighbour, the children begging or borrowing, a night's cleaning work, and the 'social' money when it comes are all fluctuating but nevertheless essential elements of a fragile safety net that is more related to surviving than planning. In this state of financial precariousness, organising and planning life, especially family life, is impossible.

Yet, in spite of what is so often said about the lives of very poor people, their existence is not a 'day-to-day' one. For families who have to live like this, budgets are actually turned towards the past. When money does come in, it is the debts that have to be paid off first, especially to people who have kept them afloat and who will keep them afloat in the future.

And there are other traps. It becomes normal for people to spend the little they do have. After weeks of going short of food, when the money arrives, parents choose to buy special treats or an elaborate birthday present for their children. Also their experience confirms that the less there is left, the better the chance of receiving an emergency payment or handout. This, too, is part of the reality of extreme poverty. Putting all efforts into keeping something back does not secure other people's help. Proving there is nothing at all does.

For individuals and families, as well as for whole communities, exclusion from representing yourself, from being able to contribute to society, from acting independently, and from financial security — all denials of fundamental rights — brings in its wake the belief that, in human terms, there is no future possible. Young couples are actually told they will not be allowed to keep any children they bring into the world.[7] Healthy school-leavers are actually informed there will never be training and work for them and are put on invalidity pensions. Families actually have to potty-train their children in public toilets because they are turned out of their accommodation during the day. Children in care are actually told their parents are monsters.

This is the grotesque and evil consequence of social exclusion. At its limit, for the most impoverished and excluded men, women and children, there is no future, humanly speaking. Healthy human relationships with neighbours, shop assistants, school teachers, hospital staff and church people are just not possible. Even relationships and solidarities with people who are closest — parents, children, brothers and sisters and friends — are distorted. At this level, the very poorest people appear to adopt for themselves the image society has of them, an image that engenders humiliation and shame, not just for a week or two, but indefinitely. When humiliation and shame are passed on from one generation to the next, they are responsible for undermining the humanity of people and for perpetuating an appearance of total apathy and defeat.

Resisting exclusion: the force of the very poor

For nearly thirty years, the ATD Fourth World Movement has been witness to the suffering of families and communities, in cities and rural areas, in developed and developing countries throughout the world. Yet everywhere, this suffering is accompanied by a resistance and protest exercised by the very poorest families against their poverty and exclusion from society. This resistance signifies the unceasing belief and determination of the very poor that life can and must get better, and it is a pointer to the way society should order its priorities so that it does. This resistance rarely takes the form of collective action. Instead, it exists as a multitude of individual efforts that are expressed in very different ways.

Non-cooperation is one of them. Parents resist pressure on them to send their children to school when they see them facing the same lack of friendship and respect they experienced as children. For their part, the children resist learning when they sense that their family is mistrusted by their teacher. Mothers fail to declare their pregnancy and avoid ante-natal care when they fear their child will be removed at birth. Adults and young people resist accepting interviews for work if they know their reading and writing will be tested.

Resistance is also creating alternative ways of doing things rather than following the official line and the proper channels. To survive financially, parents and young people on supplementary benefit take on part-time work, or sell things they collect scavenged from rubbish heaps. Resistance can be expressed as unpredictable and spontaneous violence against a society that continually puts the very poor at a disadvantage. Young people break into a new youth club that has been built on their estate without consultation with them. Parents insult the social worker whose visit is felt as a threat to the family. Resistance can be expressed as extreme servility, as an acceptance to 'go along'. Families scold their little ones in an exaggerated way in the presence of the social worker. Parents openly report neighbours to the authorities for drawing benefits illegally.

These kinds of resistance to exclusion are a permanent feature of the lives of the very poorest people, but the consequences of resisting like this are costly. Thousands of children leave school unable to read and write. Community investment in local youth facilities is withdrawn. Whole families develop the habit of playing a role. It is rare for the very poorest families to talk about the cost to them of resisting. Yet their gestures show how they deplore illiteracy in school-leavers, the deception of undeclared work, violence and the obligation to act out forced relationships with people.

The most constant form of resistance, though, the cost of which is a perpetual drain on their courage and determination, is the simple fact of keeping going in spite of all the odds. The very poorest and most harshly excluded people continue to get up in the morning, continue to face the criticism of neighbours, continue to live without heat and light, continue to manifest their love for their children that have been adopted, continue to present themselves for job interviews, continue to cope with chronic ill-health on a poor diet, continue to produce and raise children in decaying and dangerous housing, and continue to live in the constant belief that people are capable of taking their side but do not want to.

These families' daily struggle to keep going is not seen in this positive light. This fight for survival is not picked up and reinforced, not given weight or significance, and not used as a basis for over-coming poverty and exclusion by a whole community. Instead, the way of doing things, which signifies their hope and courage to make things change, is ignored, misjudged or condemned.

It is not a knowledge of the weaknesses and failings of the very poor that will enable society to combat persistent poverty or exclusion. Attempts to overcome perceived inadequacies or deficiencies, or to satisfy perceived basic needs, will not achieve this either. Persistent poverty can only be eradicated through an understanding and a reinforcement of the resistance of the very poor to their condition. The forces that the non-poor must mobilise should be allied to this resistance so that the combined efforts of the poor and non-poor succeed in liberating the very poorest people, rather than giving rise to new processes that alienate them.

If the behaviour and attitudes of the poorest people were recog-nised instead as an affirmation of what it is important to defend, then it would be possible to instigate changes in society that would benefit everyone. Their abhorrence of being dependent on benefits, or of having people in authority intrude into their private lives, for example, could promote the denouncement of these situations in a way that then makes it unthinkable and impossible that they happen to anyone.

Demonstrating these resistances and the individual and collective will of the very poor to overcome the impossibilities of their lives is the purpose of our Movement. Our experience shows that Fourth World families are capable of astonishing achievements when the conditions allow and when they are with people who have confi-dence in them. Our experience shows that they are willing to come together and demonstrate what they are doing, and want to do, to combat poverty and exclusion. They will do this if they sense that their efforts will not be ignored or deformed and will attract not new controls over their lives but increased respect for poor people everywhere.

Since 1973, we have brought the very poorest families together to support and encourage those whose lives are disintegrating. We have brought families together to speak publicly about their efforts to secure training and work for their young people. And since mid-1985, we have been bringing them together to build with their own hands pilot training workshops at Frimhurst that will help point the way towards establishing appropriate training and work opportunities for the least skilled parents, young people and children.

It is in partnership with these poorest people that society will find a way of protecting and defending human dignity and human rights, by building first and foremost on the experiences in this domain of those who have to fight every day to restore the dignity and rights that are denied to them.

Overcoming exclusion: a long-term partnership with the poorest

For anti-poverty policies and programmes to succeed amongst the very poorest people and communities, they must be designed from the outset to include them. Simply trusting that the benefits of a new social security system, a special educational programme, extended youth training provision or an innovatory housing policy will somehow rub off on those who need them most is a false and unjust use of financial and human resources. This approach not only fails to reach those most in need, but actually reinforces their sense of failure, and society's condemnation of them for not 'taking advantage' of what is being provided.

It is only by establishing a permanent partnership with the very poorest people that their efforts and society's efforts to overcome poverty and exclusion can combine and have real effect. For this partnership to develop and last, two essential conditions have to be fulfilled: first, that the poorest people can come together, clarify their ideas, make sense of their experiences, practise speaking publicly and then communicate to people around them; and second, that the non-poor, their organisations and representative bodies actively take on board these experiences, ideas and proposals and evaluate all progress with the poorest people as their reference.

The first essential condition, that Fourth World families are enabled to express themselves collectively, requires a determined and long-term commitment to finding the conditions for this to happen. It means not assuming they will find the confidence to meet with others, but going out instead to encourage them to come. It means creating an atmosphere in which everyone's view is important. It means encouraging those who begin to speak to sense immediately their responsibility for those that do not. And it means being present to the poorest people for a sufficiently long time for them to sense the genuine importance to others of what they live and express.[8]

This collective expression by and on behalf of the very poor is an essential element in a truly democratic political system. It requires that the very poorest and least articulate have the means to think through the issues that are important to them without having their own understanding of situations overridden by ideas imposed from outside or above. Committed community and pressure groups defending the interests of disadvantaged sections of society are only too familiar with the tendency of meetings and decisions to be dominated by the more articulate, or by those who bring with them their own preconceived ideas and analyses. In such groups, the least articulate are always stifled.

The second essential condition, that of the non-poor taking on board the experiences, concerns and aspirations of the poorest and establishing clear priorities in their favour, is a question of introducing them into the arena of public representation and decision-making. It means making sure that what is being discussed collectively focuses on what is being communicated most inarticulately, that it is not interpreted too quickly and that decisions are not rushed. It also means facing up to the painful realisation that a group is not nearly as representative as it had thought.

This effort has to be made by individuals, community organisations, pressure groups and political parties if this long-term partnership with the very poorest people is to be established and maintained, and if the concerns and issues that are of the most significance to them are to be taken up and acted on by society as a whole. There is no other way to combat exclusion, and to ensure that our activities, proposals and programmes do not themselves reinforce it.

References

1 From 'A Place Called Frimhurst', BBC Radio, 16 October 1980.
2 Mary O'Dwyer and Joanna Hall, 'A Legal Commentary', in *To Live in Dignity: families of the Fourth World in Europe, 1984*, the report to the conference 'The Right of Families to Live in Dignity' at the Council of Europe, November 1984.
3 Presented at the International Youth Gathering, Geneva, 28 May 1985, organised jointly by the International Movement ATD Fourth World and the International Labour Office.
4 Meeting with Peter Bottomley, Under-Secretary of State at the Department of Employment, 24 May 1985.
5 Intervention of Mrs Redegeld, International ATD Fourth World Movement, at the 71st session of the 1985 General Conference of the International Labour Organisation, Geneva, reported in the Provisional Record no 21.
6 From examples quoted in L Duquesne (ed), *An End to Injustice*, ATD Fourth World, Science and Service, 1983.
7 *Pauline: families of courage*, ATD Fourth World, Science and Service, 1984.
8 Final Evaluation Report, *Dialogue with the Fourth World*, for the Directorate General, Employment and Social Affairs, Commission of the European Communities, by ATD Fourth World, 1980.

3 Power, politics and poverty

SUE WARD

For many years now we have had full adult suffrage in this country. Everyone is free to join a political party; most people would find a trade union willing to accept them as members. In theory, therefore, political power and enfranchisement are equal across the whole population, rich and poor.

But, in fact, the rich have power above the average. It is almost a cliché to say that money confers power. Lack of money also deprives people of the chance to exercise power and influence, even at the most modest level. At one extreme, if you have no fixed abode, you are literally disenfranchised by being unable to register to vote. At a less extreme level, poverty means you are powerless against the everyday institutions you must confront — the council, the school, the hospital, a large shop.

Many people, even the affluent, feel a sense of powerlessness here — but it is much enlarged if you do not have access to a phone, time to write letters of complaint, or the fare money to go down and register that complaint.

This chapter takes the issue a stage further, however, and concentrates on the difficulties faced by a poor person who wants to be active politically or in the community. It is not suggested that this is the *most* important of the exclusions facing the poor — but it is one facet, and a neglected one.

The price of activism

Almost any sort of 'activism', that is, taking part at any level in a political group, is expensive. The methods by which policy is made and fought for, individuals selected for office, essential political work carried out, all presuppose a fair amount of money at one's independent command, over and above the amount needed simply for survival. Those without this money are marginalised. In looking at this further, the next section takes the Labour Party as an example, simply because it is the one the author knows best. There is no reason to suppose, though, that things will be any different in the other mainstream parties.

My own Labour Party branch covers a ward with an unemployment rate, in December 1985, of 15.1 per cent. Hardly any of the active members, however, are jobless. Most of them are white, well-educated and in white-collar jobs. They are also young — pensioners have complained before now that the social events are run in a style that is alien to them. The most recent social event, to illustrate this, was a cocktail party in one member's house; though crowded, it included only one person who might be called elderly.

It might be said that this is because the middle-class white activist is articulate and finds it easy to dominate any meeting. But, reinforcing this, the pattern of party activity requires money, and if you do not have it you will be unable to enter the 'magic circle' of power. The financial demands of being an active member, at branch level, can be divided into:
- the cost of becoming a member at all, and getting to the meetings;
- direct requests for money — the raffle tickets, social events, sponsored walks, collections;
- costs of socialising;
- costs of keeping up to date.

Becoming a member

The cost of becoming a member is kept down, in the Labour Party, by means of a reduced rate membership subscription for the 'unwaged'. In 1986, this is £2.50, compared to £9 for the waged. The amount involved does not seem very much — but it is a much higher proportion of the unemployed person's income than of the employed person's wage. Unemployment benefit is about 15 per cent of the average industrial wage, but the subscription is 27 per cent of the standard amount. If you are employed, but low waged, you pay the full amount.

Many trade unions have taken this point on board, and have merely nominal subscriptions for unemployed people. Some have sliding scales for the lower paid, a common practice in European unions. This has been a matter of necessity rather than choice as redundancies have cut a swathe through union ranks. Some Transport and General Workers' Union branches in areas like Liverpool, it is said, are by now almost wholly composed of unemployed members.

'Sectarian' groups expect far more from their members as a proportion of their total income. Again from necessity, though, they are rather better at providing a sliding scale for the lower paid. The Militant Tendency (which, of course, denies it is anything other than a group of newspaper readers) expects its supporters to pay over a percentage of their income each week. Since they exist within the Labour Party, this is on top of the party subscription, not instead of it.

Thousands of members in all the political parties and unions pay their subscriptions and do nothing more. To do more involves going to meetings. This brings transport costs, which may not be large for a local branch meeting in a nearby church hall. A trade union branch, though, can be several miles away, and in rural areas some people have to travel long distances. In addition, there are childcare costs, and both these factors tend to disadvantage poor women more than poor men.

Fewer women have access to a car; far more need to arrange childcare before they can go out for the evening. Their partners may not be able or willing to take on the responsibilities, or may not exist. Though much babysitting is done at sweated labour rates by schoolgirls, it still takes a sizeable chunk out of a low income. There is also the need to provide a meal, and transport home afterwards. Some groups have tried to arrange childcare rotas — for instance, with branches that meet on different nights 'twinning' to provide babysitters for each other. These rely for their success on the childless members of the groups giving sufficient priority to the issue, so that they will make the effort to link up with those with dependants — not very common in my experience.

Once one reaches the meeting, one is usually faced with a barrage of requests for money, all in theory voluntary, all difficult to resist without looking mean or, even worse, uncommitted to the cause. Raffles and socials, collections for good causes, sponsored walks, all extract from the members far more than the membership fee itself. Of course, one can explain that one is poor; that, however, results in exactly the sort of stigmatising effects that social policy-makers have pointed to as a deficiency in the field of means-tested benefits.

Political party meetings, we are often told, 'are not where the real business is done' (which is just as well for those who find them too boring to attend). The 'real business' is carried on in the pub afterwards. The meeting, by this reading, is almost the penance that the Puritan British feel they have to go through, before allowing themselves off the leash to plan, conspire and gossip over a pint. But what if you cannot afford a pint for yourself, let alone a round for your cronies? If going to the pub is beyond your means, where do you do the conspiring?

Again, if you declare your poverty, people will no doubt feel sorry for you and buy the drinks, refusing to let you take your turn in getting a round. This not only involves personal humiliation, but it also reduces the usefulness of the exercise anyway. Much of the work done in the pub consists of power-broking and the trading of favours (though not in a corrupt sense). If you are asking for support for your resolution, offering help in collecting votes for something else in return, but then have to stand by and be the passive recipient of drinks rather than the equal provider, the power relationships go awry. Neither you nor your colleagues may be consciously aware of this happening. The undercurrents, though, will be there.

Keeping in touch

Political activism also involves, even at local level, the need to keep up to date and stay in touch with organised groups within and outside the formal parties. This means reading their literature and knowing what their policies are.

Many of the groups have cheap rates for membership by unemployed people — though not for the low paid—but their publications are separately priced and often, because of low print runs, disproportionately expensive. The local public library can help — you can join the morning queue to read the *Guardian*. But it's unlikely you'll be able to while away the time reading *Marxism Today or Sanity*. Most public libraries are stronger on their subscriptions to leisure magazines than they are to political periodicals. In terms of the preoccupations of the majority of their users, this is probably correct. Fishing is a far more popular pastime than political activism. However, there is also widespread political censorship about the material libraries obtain. This is often not conscious, but in some cases it is quite deliberate — a few years ago the London Borough of Wandsworth refused to allow the GLC publication *London after the bomb* in its libraries.

Where, then, does the activist go for information? Political groups could remedy some of the deficiencies by creating their own circulation arrangements, either privately or at branch level, but they tend not to. Political activists are very bad at lending out material, largely because other political activists are very bad at giving it back. In the 'old days', that golden age of activists before the First World War, but perhaps lingering on to the Second, the assumption was that one did not have much cash for literature. So there were book boxes at Labour Party and trade union branches. The post of branch librarian was one of several into which an aspiring bureaucrat would climb. There is a proud tradition of self-help in the miners' institutes and libraries of South Wales, in which people like Aneurin Bevan gained their political education. Today, though, despite the efforts of Llafur (the Welsh Labour History Society) and a few academics, many of these libraries have been dispersed, sometimes even sold to rag and bone men, to make way for pool tables.

It is true that book*stalls* are a common sight at branch and group meetings. There will be copious supplies of the group's own literature for sale, and smaller quantities from other people. But this is for purchasing, not borrowing. The assumption is — correctly — that most activists can well afford to buy. Those who cannot,

36

though, are more excluded than ever they were when the assumption was the opposite.

Going further

If your political ambitions take you beyond the local level, the demands on your purse also escalate. You will want to go to conferences and caucus meetings, to be invited as a speaker elsewhere, to be 'seen to be there' at all the right social events.

Becoming a delegate to a conference is often easy — there is little competition. Many trade unions are reasonably generous with expenses. Judging by the lifestyle of some delegates at the conferences, at times they may be over-generous! But constituency parties, themselves strapped for cash, are not. Some do not offer expenses, some offer them but with the unspoken assumption that you will not accept. When they are offered, they tend to cover your travel and hotel only, not food, drink, or the essential socialising and collections.

For women, there is also the acute problem of childcare. Not every child wants to go to a creche for a week. If they do, the parent, usually the mother, has to finance getting the child there, feeding and entertaining him or her for the rest of the time outside the conference hours. If the child does not want to go, you must make alternative arrangements. Unless you can rely on a relative, these are likely to be expensive, and even grandparents and aunts will expect something in return, even if only a bottle of whisky or an invitation to a meal.

Invitations to speak at meetings, essential if you want to rise up the party hierarchy, rarely include offers of expenses, even when the distance travelled is long. People are usually generous — though not universally — with offers of a bed for the night, and perhaps a meal after the meeting, but not with the train fare. Anyone who aspires to be a parliamentary candidate will be faced not only with attending formal selection meetings all over the country, but also with informal gatherings, 'nursing supporters' and attending social events and bazaars to get your face known.

The price of time

The final set of costs that political activists must bear are those of time and opportunity. It is not always recognised by middle-class people how much of what they buy with their money is time. Being poor takes up an enormous amount of time and energy. You must walk to your meeting, or take three buses, rather than even the occasional taxi. You must buy cheaper, less convenient, food, or else less nourishing 'junk' food that is going to sap your energy in the long run. The food must cook slowly, and then you have to wash the dishes, rather than just switching on first the microwave and then the dishwasher. You must tramp round jumble sales and junk shops for your clothes and household equipment. You certainly can't afford someone to clean for you.

If you have children, they will be underfoot constantly, because getting them out of the way costs money. Middle-class children are engaged in a steady social round — guides or Woodcraft Folk, dancing class, watching a new video at someone else's home. This is good for them, nice for their parents, but expensive.

Nor does the affluent person have an exhausting tramp round council offices and DHSS waiting rooms hunting for means- and stamina-tested benefits. The more financial trouble you get into, the more it eats into your time. Being taken to court for non-payment of rent must be the ultimate time-wasting occupation. All this is compounded by cuts in public services that might otherwise compensate the poor — and save them time — like public transport, school meals and libraries.

Living and working conditions

Money also buys better housing and working conditions. These also affect the amount of time you have. Keeping clean, warm and fed — even just keeping going — in a damp council flat on the fourteenth floor, where the lifts don't work and the nearest supermarket is a mile away, is going to be a struggle anyway. You don't need a round of committee meetings and newspaper selling to add to it.

If you also have an arduous and dirty job, this may affect your health, and certainly will affect your ability to turn up at a meeting on time, alert and able to take part in the discussions. A computer analyst or advertising executive can leave the office early, buy a Macdonalds to eat in the car, and arrive at the meeting reasonably alert and in working clothes — a suit — which blend in with the rest. A bus driver, perhaps, at least in the Labour Party, can also turn up in uniform, because his PSV licence is almost a badge of office. But a maintenance man in greasy overalls, or a woman whose job is on the production line in a frozen chicken factory, certainly can't.

Doing a job like that means you have to go home, wash and change. Quite possibly, you will be too exhausted to go out again. Spending the day in hard manual labour does not equip you as well, physically or mentally, for an evening of Marxism or monetarism, as a day behind a desk. While you are behind the desk, you are also far more likely to be able to refresh your memory by looking through the agenda or the committee papers, to look out of the window and think out your position, to make a few phone calls to line up your supporters or, especially if you hold any sort of elected office, to sort out cases and other people's problems.

Apart from a few Victorian workplaces, and a few enlightened ones, where everyone is treated exactly the same, management tolerance of 'outside activities', however worthy, during working time decreases in a direct relationship to your level of pay and your status within the hierarchy. By and large, a far higher rate of return, in terms of the concentration of mind and body, is demanded for the lower paid person's wages than for the higher paid. There are exceptions to this. A security guard has many opportunities to stare into space and read the papers, while a brain surgeon does not. As an overall generalisation, though, it holds true.

Aisha, operating a sewing machine, and Eve, her personnel officer, may both be on the same school governors. Aisha cannot take a phone call during working hours, nor make one except from a coin box at lunchtime. She will lose pay if she sits on an interview panel for the new head. She has a right under the Employment Protection Act to unpaid time off for public duties, narrowly defined, but management is grudging about it, and if she takes too much advantage she will not be given the better piecework tasks where higher bonus can be earned. If she has a meeting stretching far into the night, as often happened when Labour Parties were tearing themselves to pieces over rate-capping, and arrives at work late the next day, she loses money and may even be disciplined.

Personnel officer Eve, in an office of her own, can take or make as many phone calls as she likes. She can probably ask her secretary to type letters, so long as she does not push her luck too far. Management won't object much if she takes the odd day for civic duties. They might even welcome it, as a way of demonstrating what a public-spirited firm they are. If Eve stays late at a meeting, she can always come into work late and, if all else fails, she can 'take a report home to finish', that well understood euphemism for taking time off in the middle of the day for some other reason.

Powerless women

All the problems here limit the power of either sex, to an extent that the wonder is that so many people persevere against the odds, rather than how few succeed. The obstacles, though, are doubled for women, for money brings power within one's own home as well as outside it, and lack of money brings greater powerlessness. Many, perhaps most, married women meet active or passive resistance from their husbands when they become politically involved. Money allows you to buy your way past that resistance, in all sorts of ways. If you can buy a babysitter's time, you can go to your branch meeting *and* your partner can go to the pub, on the same evening. So he won't resent your curtailing his activities. If you can afford to buy a week's good and interesting meals, prepare them and put them in the freezer labelled 'Monday evening', 'Tuesday lunch', and so on, you've removed the 'How can I look after myself?' barrier to going to a conference. If you have two cars, you can go to a meeting independently, and return, however late it is, without having to ask for the favour of being collected. Without the resources, the grudges and the complications build up. No wonder many women retire defeated.

There are other problems too. Low paid men in many industries work enormous amounts of overtime to bring their earnings up to a living wage. This means their wives also have to work long hours, as effective single parents with the whole responsibility of child care for that time. Unsocial hours, shift work and the twilight shift all add to the burden.

A woman not in paid work, finally, has the problem of having little or no money of her own. The child benefit book may be her only resource independent of the man's pay packet. As the recent CPAG/PPA survey showed,[1] child benefit is usually spent on necessities. Even in households with a lot of money coming in, it is often unequally shared, as Jan Pahl has shown.[2] Where there is not enough to go round, it means the non-waged partner must go through a double means test, first with her partner as she asks for cash to pay for a meeting, and then again at the meeting itself.

Very many women's jobs, even those classified as non-manual, are in the category where they demand total attention throughout. Working in a shop, nursing, on an electronic assembly line or packaging, routine clerical work in front of a word processor, are all repetitive but require concentration.

Even where you can make yourself heard and there is access to a phone, management tolerance is unconsciously conditioned, time and again, by their views of women. Office juniors will be ticked off, but not too severely, for long phone calls with or about their boy friends, but a phone call about going to Greenham Common will be heavily frowned on, as it fits the wrong stereotype.

While, in our example above, Eve, the personnel officer, may be allowed time off for 'civic duties', Mary, the senior secretary, would find it much more difficult. The secretary's role as 'office wife' means she has to be there, whether or not there is much to do, and be instantly available to bail out her boss when he loses his train ticket, needs an excuse for his failed appointment, or wants a ten-page document typed between five in the afternoon and a meeting first thing the next morning.

Solutions

Is all this inevitable, within our capitalist, class-structured system, or are there changes that can be made? In some ways, the picture is, if not inevitable, at least intrinsic to the system. If the poor gain power, a lot more will have changed than simply their ability to attend meetings. But even so, in classic reformist terms, there are things that political and campaigning groups, with a commitment to the fairer distribution of wealth and power, can do meanwhile:

• We can stop making the number of good causes you contribute to, the newspapers you buy, the conferences you attend, tests of political commitment. They are much more a test of resources, and we ought to see this.

• We can make the assumption from the start that people get their expenses, for travelling, babysitting and accommodation, if they do things for the group. Fares and expenses pools are a start, but we ought to go further and ensure that no one has to be out of pocket from their political activity.

• There is a problem, though, because this means more fund-raising to pay for it. If the whole thing is not to become a vicious circle, such fund-raising must be based on going out to non-supporters rather than simply buying each other's raffle tickets. Running a jumble sale rather than a bookstall for the converted, or having a social in a pub rather than in someone's home so that new people can be sold tickets, are politically better tactics anyway; they are also easier for the non-affluent to deal with.

• We should think more about the costs of getting to meetings, and arrange shared lifts, and take babysitting rotas more seriously. The emphasis on doing the 'real work in the pub' should be fought. If the formal meeting is so useless, then it should be either abandoned or changed, but not added to.

• Trade unions ought to put a much higher priority on obtaining decent facilities for carrying out public work. The Employment Protection Act 1975 needs to be strengthened to cover a far wider range of activities without loss of pay. If that is felt to be too great a burden to bear, then all employers could contribute to a fund, like the Maternity Pay Fund, for those with public-spirited employees to draw upon. Anyone holding an elected office should have the right of access to a phone and an office.

• Union educational work should as far as possible happen at the workplace, in working time.

• Once the legal rights have been achieved, council meetings and other political meetings ought to happen during the day, not to cut so hard into people's evenings and weekends.

Finally, those concerned with writing policy, at any level and in any group, should think as much about *access* to provision as about the provision itself. If they are to alter the powerlessness of the poor, it needs positive action, not simply an assumption that the poor will find a way through somehow. This means, it does need stressing, the middle classes handing over some of their power, in political parties as much as anywhere else.

References

1   Alison Walsh and Ruth Lister, *Mother's Lifeline: a survey of how women use and value child benefit*, CPAG/PPA, 1985.
3   Jan Pahl, 'Who benefits from Child Benefit?', *New Society*, 25 May 1985.

4 Playing away from home: leisure, disadvantage and issues of income and access

ALAN TOMLINSON

It is in the world of leisure, away from the home, that the divide between the privileged and the poor now finds one of its most observable public forms. Consumers have emerged as a new kind of 'leisure class'. Raymond Williams has captured a central characteristic of this consumer culture in his idea of 'mobile privatisation'.[1] By this he means that more and more, in the world of leisure, people have chosen to do things in immediate social groups, or on their own. They will go 'out' when it pleases them. Improvements in transport and communication, increased private car ownership and improved road networks have made much of this possible. It all backfires, sometimes, in the motorway jams, in fraught social relations inside the over-full car on the Bank Holiday weekend. But people pack up and set off again next Bank Holiday, making individual decisions about where to go and what to do — what's the latest spectacle, where haven't we been yet, 'Mum, Dad, the telly says we should go...'.

There's plenty to do, we're reminded, as a consumer. And the images in Sunday supplements and other forms of media advertising constantly urge us to do it. In consuming and spending, we do our little bit to boost the flagging economy; our leisure becomes in turn productive. But many people have little opportunity to express such consumer choice. Such people are doubly disadvantaged. Denied the basic requirements of the consumer — regular work and disposable income — they are also excluded from the 'leisure lifestyle'. Not admitted in the first place, they are then branded by their exclusion. Yet talk of the new 'leisure society' conjures up images of a world of limitless possibilities for those with time on their hands, but little money in their pockets. Clearly, their possibilities will be very different from those open to the more economically privileged.

Idle time and useful leisure

Leisure has always been determined by power and privilege. The world of leisure has been a world of inequality as much as of opportunity. It has also been a sphere in which disputes over what

43

is 'acceptable behaviour' have been prominent. Not infrequently, leisure has been seen very openly as a means of transforming the consciousness of the populace. In the nineteenth century the 'rational recreation' movement attempted to 'civilise' the more boisterous elements in working-class popular culture, to formalise and standardise leisure activities in ways that would make them 'self-improving'. Ideologues from the churches and from the newly emergent commercial bourgeoisie formed alliances to attack certain notions of leisure as dangerous and to attempt, through leisure, to achieve forms of class conciliation. Arguments and conflicts concerning 'time' have often been linked to the question of leisure. E P Thompson showed clearly how the industrial worker's unproductive use of time (when not occupying measured time at work) was of great concern to the urban bourgeoisie. He quotes the views of one 1821 moralist, on manual workers left with:

> . . . several hours in the day to be spent nearly as they please. And in what manner . . . is this precious time expended by those of no mental cultivation? We shall often see them just simply annihilating these portions of time. They will for an hour, or for two hours together . . . sit on a bench or lie down on a bank or hillock . . . yielded up to utter vacancy and torpor . . . [2]

It is this sort of concern which is at the heart of some contemporary debates about the 'problem' of leisure, a century and a half on. The unconstructive use of public space is still seen as threatening. The question of how time and public space are used — idly or constructively, rationally — has been a recurrent one in the modern period.

But as recently as the 1920s and the 1930s, the work-leisure relationship was pretty blurred, very different in a traditional working-class experience from that in the burgeoning middle-class suburban culture. People lived and worked in working-class neighbourhoods and communities which offered a rich texture to their everyday lives — maybe not much in terms of material comforts, and often virtually nothing in terms of conspicuous consumption. But accounts of life in the inter-war period show us that, despite the rosy glow of the popular memory that might idealise such conditions of living, neighbourhood and community were still important contexts for leisure. Local, collective and often self-generated activities still thrived. At the same time, the embryonic consumer culture was under construction in the rise of suburban culture: radios, cars, fashion, holidays, paperbacks. Consumer horizons were certainly expanding, but not for everyone. Spectator sport was popular, but not always for the spectacle. Alun Howkins has pointed out that admission to Lords cricket ground in the 1930s was one of the cheapest ways of getting a seat for the day if you were unemployed, with nowhere to go and limited options about what to do.[3]

'Idle' time, it has often been thought, could be made respectable — and therefore less threatening — if turned into 'leisure' time. In the 1980s in Britain, the same issues are being raised. 'New' notions of discipline, around concerns of time and work, are being debated. This is one new form of a very old problem for a dominant culture seeking to hold on to its dominance: how to speak to diverse elements in the society and to convince them of their integral place in that society. Unemployed youth with little spending power and no options in the leisure market will understandably be sceptical about such attempts. People labouring away at cleaning offices in the early mornings of grey, cold autumn days; underpaid hirelings of multinational fast-food chains; non-unionised employees of rurally splendid theme parks; disgracefully paid waitresses with only temporary and casual work; invisible labourers cleaning up the refuse of the consumer society at play — all these figures, bent and exploited presences in the consumer landscape, whose role is so necessary as service labour to the consumer 'leisure class' — all these will also be sceptical about the claims that we are a 'united society' in which the individual is free to choose, able to determine his or her own destiny.

Two nations of leisure

For we are not just free agents in the social world. Options as to what we do away from home will be open, or limited, to us on the basis of a number of things: money, time, desire, confidence. And we will respond to possibilities differently in terms of our class, age, gender or race. Just because resources or facilities are there is no guarantee that they are accessible to all. Take the example of the squash court, one of the booming leisure activities of the 1960s/70s. Recent figures have shown this to be one of the most evenly distributed of male sports activities across the age range. Though 'regular' squash is played most among males between the ages of 20 and 34 (1 in 10), 7 per cent or so of 16-19-year-old males, and 4 per cent or so of 35-59-year-olds polled played regularly. Given what the Henley Centre for Forecasting describes as the 'large body of people who remain unconvinced of the attractions of sport',[4] this looks like a pretty steady and evenly distributed participation rate in squash. But let's look more closely at who might be playing, and how they go about fitting squash into their lifestyle. Other figures have shown the class bases of participation. Clearly, 'male', in the Henley Centre's use of the Central Statistical Office's figures, is a very undeveloped category. 'White, suburban, middle-class professional male' might be a more

45

adequate expanded category. Buying kit, shoes, racket, balls, and paying fees and so on are premised on adequate disposable income. United Kingdom spending on sports clothing and footwear has risen from an estimated £275m in 1979 to a quite staggering £780m in 1984 — a massive increase.

All sorts of developments may have fed into such an increase — for instance, the school gates of many well-to-do neighbourhoods have become informal fashion paradegrounds, mostly for women's 'leisure' or 'jogging' fashions during the last few years of the 'body boom'. But we know that the increase in squash playing has drawn in people who are able to spend on sports clothing and footwear. Looking good, not just feeling good, has been a central concern of people contributing to the physical renaissance that is evident in a few boom sports. And, quite simply, this has cost money!

Also, less obvious but of equal importance, getting on court is no simple matter. Where squash has boomed, you might need a telephone, a diary, some flexible working hours, as well as all the kit, before starting. The squash game is set up just like the business meeting. Punctuality; precision; short, sharp and decisive action; the game often needs to be set up organisationally, played promptly and somewhat privately. It is the leisure activity *par excellence* for the thrusting young professional. But if you work on a factory floor for a set number of clocked-in hours, or if you are unemployed and have no phone to hand, even the basic requirements to booking are not part of your cultural repertoire. Leisure is not and never has been a social space wide open to any newcomer.

The world of leisure has never been open and accessible in this way. The professional forecasters, high-tech crystal-ball gazers of the Henley Centre don't mince their words on this: 'The *"Two Nations"* phenomenon is becoming more pronounced and will continue to do so for the foreseeable future.'[5] They then offer several dimensions along which the 'two nations' phenomenon can be seen: north vs south; poor vs rich; unemployed vs employed, tenant vs occupier; youth vs non-youth; urban vs rural. Yet, around most of these dimensions, it is the accessibility of different groups to commodity culture which is the major dividing line between the privileged and the poor. The culture of consumption in leisure is becoming increasingly remote and impossible a prospect for those excluded by both social and economic disadvantage. 'Mobile privatisation' might have become a significant aspect of the contemporary culture of consumption for some, but it is clear that many groups and individuals are unable even to consider the option of following the trend. Leisure activities are not the product of free individual choices made in a social world of wide-open possibilities.

Away-from-home activities are not, apart from motoring,

dominant among younger age groups. Eating out has increased in recent years, but very much in terms of overseas tourist markets and fast-food expenditure. And the latter, as any parent of young children knows, is hard to see as leisure rather than familial obligation. The top five away-from-home entertainments, in the Henley Centre's recent time-use survey, are the pub (surely one of the longest reigning chart-toppers of all time), motoring, dance-clubs/discos, sports clubs and the cinema. Age is a big factor here. Young adults make up a high proportion of pub-goers and, not surprisingly, of dancers. As we look at figures for dance-activity through the life cycle, there is a dramatic fall-off after middle age — so, too, with sports clubs, though not so dramatically. And, perhaps more surprisingly, there is the same trend in cinema attendance. The general pattern to emerge from close consideration of the top five examples of 'playing' away from home is clear enough: after early adulthood more and more people spend more and more of their spare time in and around the house. Televisions, gardens, home improvements, home screenings, home entertaining. These constitute the core elements in a consumer culture which develops the home as self-governed leisure centre.

But leisure activities outside the home have clear boundaries formed by class and gender, not just age. It is not simply 'women' who play bingo — which attracts 13 per cent of women — it is middle-aged to elderly working-class women. And much of the drinking in pubs throughout the land — as any early evening commuter pint-drinker will know — is by males. Motoring is perhaps the activity most evenly distributed across age bands, with a slight peak amongst people in the 46-55 age groups — driving around, maybe, with a new sense of freedom, now that the children are no longer with them!

Generally speaking, the most obviously growing parts of the leisure market seem to be sports clubs and the pub. For the sports club, the potential member needs, as noted earlier with reference to squash-playing, a range of cultural competencies, as well as money. For the pub, money is always needed. Other 'growth' areas include theme parks, the death-knell for the ties of community and neighbourhood which were at the heart of earlier experiences of free-time and leisure. Alton Towers is clean, tidy, efficient, good fun undeniably. It is also functional, crowded, anonymity-inducing, slick. And for an average size family it could easily run to £40 or £50 for the day. What better image of unequal access in leisure than this: an ancient country house in remote Derbyshire countryside catering for the hedonistic needs of suburban crowds, whilst an increasing proportion of the country's urban population wonders how it might eke out the basis of subsistence.

It is worth taking a look at the stark facts of consumer ownership and of leisure participation. Although in some senses increasingly sophisticated forms of mass production have made a range of consumer goods available at relatively accessible prices, that accessibility is far from universal. There has certainly been an increase in the domestic availability of the telephone. In 1973, only 45 per cent of all households had one. In 1984, 78 per cent of households could boast this vital form of communication with the outside world — a sizeable increase, but still leaving almost a quarter of all households without one. Proportionately, more owner-occupiers than tenants have had telephones. A car, vital for so many forms of leisure, was owned in 1983 by only around half of households (the figures on this vary, from 43 to 59 per cent). Of the tenants of local authorities and new towns in 1983, only 29 per cent had a car available.[6]

Much leisure away from home — note the pervasiveness of the credit card and cheque card notices in restaurants, cinemas, shops, petrol stations and transport termini — is premised on formalised personal finances. But, as Jan Toporowski's chapter in this pamphlet shows, only a minority of poorer households have bank accounts or access to financial aids and institutions.

The inequality of participation in leisure activities is starkly displayed in Table 1. In only dancing, drinking and attendance at fairs (deep-rooted traditional activities in working-class as well as youth culture) is there a significantly even participation rate by different socio-economic groups. In most cases, activity increases proportionately with income.

'But everyone at least gets a holiday', it might be objected, in the age of paid holidays. But you are only paid if you have work. And there are many examples of paid work which leaves little room for expenditure on leisure. So even having a break away from home is far from a general trend — 42 per cent of adult residents of Great Britain took no holiday in 1983. More people have taken more than one holiday a year throughout the last decade, but these have been those for whom the holiday is already part of their social calendar; they have simply chosen to get away more. The leisured get more leisure, while the rest stay at home. As *Social Trends* puts it: 'In 1983 58% of adults in social classes D and E did not have a holiday compared with only 22% in classes A and B; over a third of those in classes A and B, but only 11% in classes D and E, had more than one holiday.'

Those already immersed in a consumer-based leisure culture, those already 'doing the business', know exactly what's what. Leisure becomes a public statement of status and relative privilege. It stresses exclusivity quite as much as open opportunity. Roger Daltry is the spokesperson for those riding high on the wave of consumer leisure: 'This does the business. The American Express card shows exactly who's who.'

Table 1: Participation[1] in selected social and cultural activities in Great Britain: by socio-economic group[2] and by sex, 1983 (%)

	Professional employers and managers	Intermediate and junior non-manual	Skilled manual and own account non-professional	Semi-skilled and unskilled manual	Full-time students	All persons[3]	All males[3]	All females[3]
Percentage in each group engaging in each activity in the 4 weeks before interview								
Open air outings								
seaside	9	9	6	6	6	7	7	8
country	5	3	2	2	2	3	3	3
parks	4	5	3	3	2	4	3	4
Entertainment, social, and cultural activities								
going to the cinema	9	10	5	4	27	7	7	8
visiting historic buildings	13	11	6	5	7	8	8	8
going to the theatre/opera/ballet	8	7	2	2	7	4	4	5
going to museums/art galleries	5	4	2	2	4	3	3	3
amateur music/drama	4	4	2	2	11	3	3	3
attending leisure classes	3	3	1	1	1	3	3	3
going to fairs/amusement arcades	1	2	1	1	2	1	1	2
going out for a meal[4]	61	51	34	27	46	40	41	40
going out for a drink[4]	56	55	61	50	61	54	64	46
dancing	10	13	9	9	31	11	10	12
Home-based activities								
listening to records/tapes[4]	69	70	60	54	93	63	65	62
gardening[4]	58	47	46	39	20	44	50	39
needlework/knitting[4]	14	42	11	30	22	27	2	48
house repairs/DIY[4]	55	35	45	27	22	36	51	24
reading books[4]	68	70	44	45	74	56	50	61
Sample size (= 100%) (numbers)	2,391	5,632	4,115	5,658	550	19,070	8,751	10,319

1 Annual averages of participation of people aged 16 or over. 2 full-time students are covered separately. 3 Includes armed forces, and persons who have never worked. These are excluded from the analysis by socio-economic group. 4 The high participation levels are partly attributable to the fact that these items were prompted.

Source: Social Trends, 15, 1985, Table 10.3.

Exclusion from the leisure utopia

In a very important social document on the life of young people in Wolverhampton in the mid-1980s, we see a social world far removed from the consumer world, a very different cultural landscape indeed.[7] There are no neat work/leisure distinctions here, no tidy categories of leisure activities. Young people in Wolverhampton know what they want: they want work. For that is what provides the promise of consumerism, to play one's part in the cycle of production-consumption. Denied their role at the point of production, many young and unemployed people today are also disqualified from participation at the point of consumption. Doubly disadvantaged, such young people as those studied by Paul Willis and his collaborators in this report make up a population of the excluded.

They know what they want to do, but are unable to do it if they are unemployed or underpaid. They want to drink, buy clothes and music. The most common activities among those in the study's sample (a mixture of employed and unemployed youth) who had visited the town centre during the day were shopping and window-shopping, meeting friends, using the library, and 'signing on', and then going to the pub, to the job-centre, and 'hanging about'. There is not a lot about sports clubs, and even pubs do not feature high, in this picture of inner-city leisure culture among the young.

As Paul Willis points out, when we look closely at the current experience of inner-city youth, it is clear that 'for the first time in modern history, a whole social group face the prospect of the effective disappearance of work and the wage for a very prolonged period'[8] — perhaps, for some, for the whole of their lives. No amount of palliatives will make 'leisure' a substitute for work, when the full promise of leisure is premised upon the power of the consumer in the market place. And once we recognise the specificity of different groups' experience, the problem is compounded still further. Unemployed black youth in Wolverhampton are particularly disenfranchised from the leisure democracy:

> The high level of unemployment within the black community makes leisure facilities an important factor... There are no real social leisure or formal leisure pursuits which are relevant for young blacks in Wolverhampton. Social leisure pursuits such as discos, pubs and other evening adult meeting places, or formal leisure pursuits such as institutionalised activities, mainstream youth clubs and unemployed activities do not attract young blacks. They concentrate, therefore, on activities with an acceptable cultural content where they feel more comfortable.[9]

A full and adequate grasp of the diversity of the experience of different groups reveals different scales of exclusion from the leisure utopia. But, in the last instance, the divide is clearly between two unequally positioned cultures. And when well-meaning initiatives to open up access to the underprivileged are made, the consequences are far from the ones anticipated by the well-intentioned leisure provider. Two examples illustrate this, both also showing the importance of definitions of time.

In sport and leisure centres throughout the land, schemes for ease of access of the unemployed to the facilities have met with mixed response. Conceived very much as contemporary forms of 'improving' initiatives which will solve the problem of 'idle time' among non-productive people, they have been unevenly and sometimes naively developed. And they have in a very real sense been imposed. One survey of schemes provided for the unemployed by local authorities revealed that only six out of 285 respondents made any systematic attempts, 'either before or after launching a scheme, to assess the likely wants of the intended customers'.[10] Most attempts at provision were much more rooted in 'faith' and 'hunch' than in any coherently developed view of what the relationship of the unemployed is to the 'leisure society'. 'Traces of obligation and haste, rather than enthusiasm and positive planning' were said by Sue Glyptis to be characteristic of this 'hasty initiative'.[11]

To counter this, pre-launch surveys of interests have been recommended.[12] But such a strategy, a form of market-research on the under-privileged, would have to break with the tradition of the provider mentality. Too often, 'sport and leisure for the unemployed' has been a slogan for keeping what providers see as potential trouble-makers off the streets. Although more progressive authorities — the Greater London Council (before its demise) and Sheffield, for instance — have sought not to impose 'wants' from above, concessionary rates in prescribed times can only be the wooden spoon in the competitive consumer society. The general trends work against the success of such schemes anyway, when public provision — be this in terms of libraries or playing fields — is fast being eroded, to be replaced by expensive private provision. In the 'mixed economy' of leisure, authorities in the affluent south-east have been the most likely not to bother to run schemes at all. Again, the leisure society is clearly an unequally accessible and a divided one.

But we should hardly be surprised that the unemployed do not always jump with joy at the offer, even when it is made. Some studies have shown how the psychological effect of unemployment has been to drive individuals into privatised retreat, into hiding in the home. Playing badminton or swimming at a cheaper rate in off-peak time on the basis of your UB40 is a pretty public declaration of your partial, marginal membership of the consumer/leisure culture; it is to accept the wearing of a badge of exclusion, to be granted access as stigma. On the municipal golf courses of Sheffield City Council, it is told, as we move towards the second millenium in a modern sophisticated civilisation, that there are fist fights on the greens. Unemployed, given access, play the course in truly leisured style, taking their time. Employed players must hurry; time is money; work beckons. Rather than 'Playing through, please', the greeting from one foursome of employed drivers to another group of leisurely-paced out-of-work players is more likely to be: 'Get out of the way, you idle buggers!'

Freedom, free-time, and the leisure myth

We live in a society in which we are said to be free to make our own choices. We choose our husbands, wives, lovers, television channels, newspapers, politicians. The freedom to choose, we are told, is a central principle of liberal democratic societies.

This conflation of 'freedom of choice' and 'individualism' is the core of the New Right's ideological grip in this moment of crisis in welfare democracy.[13] For the majority of the British working people are still in work; Thatchernomics claims to have conquered inflation: consumer goodies are cheaper, swisher and more and more accessible. 'Don't leave home without it', we are reminded by some of the most reactionary popular figures of the day — Sevy Ballesteros, for instance. And so many don't: with Amex or Visa or Mastercard snugly tucked into their credit card wallets, armed for active service on the consumer battlefields of western capitalism. Within all of this, leisure is presented as the sphere in which individual freedoms are expressed (you can do what you want), and in which badges of individual success can be displayed (the new suit, the Sony Walkman) in public declarations of privatised living.

And for the unemployed, the poorly paid, the disadvantaged, there is always hope. For if Alan Sugar did it, why not me? If the millionaire electrical chain-store dealer started with just one barrow and a couple of cardboard boxes of stock, then who can deny the New Right's claim that freedom to succeed is there, if only the individual tries hard enough.

There are, of course, many ways of opposing and contesting this view of things. Choices only exist in contexts. Those contexts are ones in which relations of power and privilege determine how much freedom we actually have in the choices we make. We will not be very likely to make our million if we come from an ethnic inner-city neighbourhood, where work itself is not part of our experience, where the idea of 'working' for wages is a merely abstract principle, where you and your mates may never have worked in your life. This is the converse side of the Amex vision of life, of Roger Daltry's call to us to make sure that we 'don't leave home without it'. Ideologue of youthful counter-cultural assertion in the 1960s/70s, Daltry is now speaking to and for the 'yuppie' generation whose world is so far apart from the dislocated world of the poor, the unemployed, the underprivileged. Structural shifts in the balance between work and leisure in the contemporary period have produced a divide of massive significance between a glossy, vibrant and conspicuous culture of consumption, and a shadowy culture of dislocation and exclusion. When these cultures meet, in the dark and violent nights of disturbance in the inner-city, in the broken windows and looted shelves of video-cassette recorder stores, the myth of the New Right's ideology of opportunity is shattered. In the desperate plight of the inner-city, in the exclusion of so many from the 'leisure society', this cultural collision finds its most dramatic form.

Unemployment figures show pretty clearly the extent of changes in the work structures of industrial capitalism. At the end of 1984, one estimate put the number of unemployed (seen as those seeking work) in western industrialised nations at 31.2 million. It is still possible to put to one side the 1 in 7 or 8 in, say, the United Kingdom, to say that they are the exception, the atypical. But when the figures are taken on a world scale, we find that the 1 in 10, or 1 in 6, or 1 in 7 add up, within the industrial system conceived worldwide, to a figure bigger than the population of a number of individual countries. Unemployment looks to be a structural feature of contemporary industrial society. Figures for the end of 1984 mark out Japan (2.7%) and Sweden (3%) as prominent exceptions to the general rule; but the Netherlands (17%), United Kingdom (13.9%), Canada (11.2%), West Germany (10.6%), France (10.3%) and Italy (10%) demonstrate the scale of the problem. And grasping this as a structural feature of contemporary societies, it becomes clear that a consumer culture of leisure is a mark of a great social and economic divide. The unemployed and the poor will not be written to by Roger Daltry's sponsors. Plastic money is only a prospect for those with plenty. Here we see once more the falsity of the pluralist notion of free choice and open opportunity in leisure. In the public spaces of leisure we see the incompatibility of a buoyant consumer culture (in which time is money and pleasure is consumption) with a culture of deprivation and, ultimately, exclusion experienced by a substantial and growing proportion of the population.

References
1   R Williams, *Towards 2000*, Chatto and Windus, 1983.
2   E P Thompson, 'Time, discipline and industrial capitalism', in *Past and Present*, No 38, 1967.

3   J Lowerson and A Howkins, 'Leisure in the thirties', in A Tomlinson (ed), *Leisure and social control*, Brighton Polytechnic, 1981, p 89.
4   *Leisure Futures*, Autumn 1985, p 87.
5   As note 4 above, p 3.
6   Central Statistical Office, *Social Trends*, 15, 1985, Table 6.12, p 99.
7   P Willis et al, *The social condition of young people in Wolverhampton in 1984*, Wolverhampton Borough Council, 1985.
8   As note 7 above, p 1.
9   As note 7 above, p 86.
10 Sue Glyptis, 'Business as usual? leisure provision for the unemployed', *Leisure Studies*, Vol 2, no 3, September 1983, p 296.
11 As note 10 above, p 295.
12 S Glyptis and A C Riddington, *'Sport for the Unemployed': a review of local authority projects*, Sports Council Research Working Paper, 21, nd.
13 See D Bull and P Wilding, *Thatcherism and the Poor*, CPAG, 1983.

5 Beyond banking: financial institutions and the poor

JAN TOPOROWSKI

'That foundst me poor at first, and keepst me so.'

O Goldsmith

Traditionally in Britain, financial firms have been part of an elaborate structure in which they have performed their services with ritual and mystique. Those services have been differentiated according to the function performed and the class of person served. Only a minority of the population ever had direct dealings with financial firms, over and above merely depositing and withdrawing their savings. All this is now changing in what seems set to be the most radical reform of the financial system since the Second World War. Financial firms have been entering each others' markets, some traditional markets are being eliminated and new ones are being organised, in a regulatory atmosphere of laissez-faire. In society at large, people who in the past would never have done business with financial firms are now being rapidly and variously forced, cajoled and induced into using their services.

The latter is a change of fundamental importance. For as long as financial firms served corporate markets and the better-off, and the less well-off had their own special institutions of mutual assistance, the burden of any iniquities in the operations of those firms fell, by and large, upon those more than capable of bearing it. Now, however, all the population has become potentially the market for all financial firms. As the incomes, savings and financial transactions of most households are now cycled through increasingly commercial financial firms, the quality, cost and benefits of their services are coming to have a fundamental effect upon the expenditure patterns of the less well-off, and the latter's ability to accumulate the savings necessary to withstand downturns in income and the arrival of large bills. At the same time, those excluded from financial markets, who are mainly the poor, have the disadvantage of their poverty compounded by their inability to perform what have become quite elementary financial transactions.

Banks and building societies

Among financial services, the most basic ones for all classes in society are undoubtedly those that are usually placed in the category of banking services. Banking is a simple, secure and convenient way of distributing income to those with accounts in the clearing bank system. It is the simplest and most direct way, in an increasingly cashless economy, of encashing non-cash credits or income. Thirdly, the clearing arrangements of the banking system provide a secure and straightforward way of arranging payments to other account holders.

In the past, the clearing banks also looked after the liquid savings (ie, those capable of being drawn upon at short notice) of their customers. In the context of this chapter, savings should be thought of as the facility to postpone or (in the case of, say, hire purchase) advance expenditure beyond the constraints of current income — the notion that savings are a means of self-enrichment is merely an arriviste conceit.

In the early 1960s, personal deposits with banks exceeded those with building societies (the other major savings vehicle) by almost a half. Since then, however, the liquid savings of the personal sector (ie, of persons and households, as opposed to corporate bodies and the government) have for tax and other reasons been attracted increasingly to the building societies. By 1970, the banks and the building societies were virtually level. By the end of 1984, the building societies' deposits were 54 per cent greater than those of the banks.

Table 1: *Personal sector deposits 1970-84* (£m)

	Banks	Building societies	National Savings
1970	10,062	10,059	2,518
1978	24,490	36,616	3,509
1983	54,804	77,243	6,030
1984 (provisional)	58,641	90,365	6,560

Source: Financial Statistics
Note: These figures show overall trends. Due to changes in the definition of the banks and national savings, these statistics are not consistent throughout the period shown.

The National Savings movement, as Table 1 shows, does not play a major part in society's personal savings overall. Nevertheless, it is an important sector because National Savings has traditionally been the main repository for the short-term savings of those such as women, the poor and the elderly, who are still largely excluded from the markets of commercial financial institutions. The relative unimportance of National Savings reflects in part the relative unimportance, in financial terms, of its customers. In any case, for the banks personal sector savings are no longer as important as they once were, having been to a great degree replaced by the deposits of companies and inter-bank borrowing.

Table 2 gives a profile by income of those who have bank and building society accounts, based on market research surveys conducted in 1984 and 1985. As with all financial and survey statistics, care should be taken not to interpret them too literally. In this particular case, this is because of the high proportion of respondents who would not admit which income group they belonged to. However, broadly speaking, the higher a person's income, the more likely that person is to have a bank account and a building society account.

Table 2: *The income distribution of banking accounts*

Annual income	% of adults with clearing bank current account	% of clearing bank current holders in income class	% of adults with building society account	% of building holders in income class
Income not stated	41.0	11.6	31.1	11.2
£2,999 or less	48.7	9.3	37.8	9.2
£3,000 to £4,999	65.2	10.8	49.5	10.4
£5,000 to £6,999	74.9	12.1	55.9	11.6
£7,000 to £8,999	81.5	12.7	63.7	12.7
£9,000 to £10,999	85.2	12.3	66.9	12.3
£11,000 to £14,999	89.0	15.5	71.1	15.8
£15,000 and over	88.7	15.7	74.3	16.8

Source: Target Group Index, BRMB © 1985

In general, although there seem to be fewer adults with building society accounts than with bank accounts, the income of building society customers is not significantly less than that of bank customers. This would seem to belie, or at least qualify substantially, the oft-repeated claim that building societies are friendly and accessible institutions catering for the financial needs of humbler members of society who have been frightened off by the grandeur of the main clearing banks. In their functioning, too, building societies may be said to mobilise the savings of the broad mass of the saving public in order to provide that mainspring of upward economic mobility that home ownership nowadays is for the middle classes.

However, as the marketing managers of all financial institutions would not be slow to point out, income is not the major determinant of the use of particular financial services. Wealth, that is the stock of property owned by a person or a household, may be just as important, and great wealth, as our landed aristocracy lament, does not necessarily entail great income. Even more important is the *style* of life and financial acumen. These are most often determined in turn by a person's occupation or, more broadly, their socio-economic status (ie, the status of their work). The relationship between this and ownership of bank and building society accounts is summarised in Table 3. This shows that only just over two-thirds of all adults have a clearing bank current account, and only just over a half have a building society account. More men than women have these accounts.

Table 3: *The social distribution of banking accounts (%)*

	Clearing bank current account	Building society account
All adults	68.8	54.0
Men	72.6	56.6
Women	65.4	51.6
Social class		
AB	88.2	71.3
C1	81.8	63.1
C2	69.2	53.4
D	56.3	45.2
E	41.1	31.6

Source: Target Group Index, BRMB © 1985

Unfortunately, this market research study did not survey holdings of National Savings ordinary accounts. Had it done so, it is likely to have shown that this account is most popular with women and the less well-off, who are over-represented among the 10 per cent of the adult population which has National Savings accounts.

Table 3 also shows bank and building society accounts to be most popular with the higher socio-economic status groups, ie, among professional and managerial people and their families. In group E, defined as 'those at the lowest levels of subsistence', where the head of the household is a state pensioner, widow, or a 'casual or lower-grade worker', only a minority have current bank and building society accounts.

Because of the crucial role that current account banking plays in facilitating the receipt and payment of income, it is worth looking at who it is that does not have a bank account. The social profile of this group in the population, numbering some 15½ million persons, is shown in Table 4. Thus, over a third of women do not have a bank account, compared with just over a quarter of all men.

The majority of adults in social class E have no bank account, as also do the majority of those with incomes of less than £3,000 per year (roughly under £60 per week).

Table 4: *The unbanked*

% of adults without a current (cheque-book) account

All adults	31.2	*Income group*	
All men	27.4	Not stated	59.0
All women	34.6	£2,999 or less	51.3
Social class		£3,000 to £4,999	34.8
AB	11.8	£5,000 to £6,999	25.1
C1	18.2	£7,000 to £8,999	18.5
C2	30.8	£9,000 to £10,999	14.8
D	43.7	£11,000 to £14,999	11.0
E	58.7	£15,000 and over	11.3

Source: Target Group Index, BRMB © 1985

Therefore, most of the unbanked are women. A majority of them are in social classes D (ie, the unskilled and semi-skilled manual workers and their families) and E, and a majority of them probably have incomes of less than £100 per week.

Why is it that women, the less well-off, and the marginally employed make such little use of banking facilities? Do they exclude themselves or are they excluded? In the case of unbanked women, an important factor is undoubtedly economic dependence on a male breadwinner, who also operates a bank account on behalf of the family. However, women do form the majority of holders of National Savings Bank Ordinary Accounts, which gives them access to rudimentary banking services through post offices and sub-post offices.

Traditionally, the less well-off have been excluded from the clearing bank system in the United Kingdom (although less so in Scotland). This used to be done by requiring aspiring account holders to deposit a relatively large sum of money with the bank, or provide references, in order to obtain banking facilities. From the late 1960s until 1985, charges were levied on accounts when the balance in them fell below a certain amount, ranging from £100 for most banks, to £1,000 for the 'top person's' bank Coutts. Nowadays, 'down-market' customers are discouraged informally by restricting their access to banking services, and formally by limiting the range of services to which they are entitled.

Inconvenience in the use of banking facilities is created by situating bank branches mainly in the commercial centres of urban areas. This reflects the relatively greater importance to banks of commercial, as opposed to personal, business. However, it also tends to make access more difficult for those living in rural areas, or the elderly, unemployed, or housebound, who are more confined to suburban housing estates. It is this kind of inaccessibility that could be reduced significantly by 'electronic banking' direct from the home to the bank. Whether it will alter the unfavourable position of the unbanked will be discussed in the final section of this chapter. However, it should be pointed out here that the problem of the geographic distribution of bank branches is getting worse as greater competition is forcing clearing banks to shut down branches outside the main commercial centres.

A second factor in the inaccessibility of banking is the limited hours of opening, summed up in the phrase '9.30 until 3.30, with long queues at lunch-time, and never on a Saturday'. Again, for commercial customers settling their affairs by messenger, these hours hardly constitute any inhibition to business. But for many ordinary people working by the clock and with one-hour lunch-breaks between 12 and 2 o'clock, the incommodiousness of these hours really is discouraging. With greater competition recently from building societies that have started offering more effective banking services, the major clearing banks are starting to open some of their branches on Saturdays. However, on the whole, these are only in commercial centres and offer limited services on that day, concentrating on foreign exchange facilities, and the sale of fee-earning services, rather than ordinary cash withdrawal and payments' transmission services.

The third, and what is for some by no means the most insignificant factor, is the august air of mystery that our society throws over banking and finance. For those born into families that use banking facilities, their secrets are easily passed on. For those who are not so fortunate, banking and banks remain a mystery and an intimidating one at that: banks are seen as the servants of the upper classes, government and commerce, who daily torment the poor and the ignorant, and who are suspected by them (with some justice on occasion) of robbing and swindling them. Recent studies have shown that the less well-off or, more specifically, those in the lower socio-economic status groups (D and E) find banks and banking procedures daunting, when not actually frightening. On the whole, they tend to find building societies less intimidating. This is one of the arguments for the development of banking services by building societies and finance houses.[1]

A major feature of the system of bank charges, finally swept away by inter-bank competition in 1985, was that it concentrated payments for using cheque-books on those who could not afford (or were too careless) to keep £100-£150 in their current accounts.

A second characteristic that made it still more uncongenial to the poor was its unpredictability. It was not possible, and still remains so for many financial services, to know at the time of use (eg, when issuing a cheque) the actual cost of the transaction. For those living a financially precarious existence, buying a service at an unknown cost can be the prelude to financial and personal catastrophe. Apart from the interest that they charge, which they are now obliged by law to reveal, most banks still do not make clear to their customers many of the fees that they charge.

Information about the actual money cost of transactions is crucial because, in their struggle for survival in a world of beguiling financial snares, the less well-off and least financially astute are forced to employ one tactic and one criterion for assessing financial commitments. This is to examine the present and total cash cost in relation to present and future cash income. Hence the preference of the less well-off for the metered use of electricity, gas, telephone and television facilities, despite their actual higher cost and financial inefficiency. It also accounts for their tendency to assess HP and credit arrangements according to the total amount to be paid in relation to their income. In this way they judge whether they can 'afford' the offer. This crude calculation enables less scrupulous financial firms and their salesmen to inflict on the poor truly outrageous rates of interest.

Under the most recent regulations, passed under the 1974 Consumer Credit Act, the actual rate of interest paid for credit has to be brought to the attention of potential borrowers. However, it is unlikely that this will make much difference to the discrimination with which the poor borrow (or save), simply because their criterion of judgment remains largely the cash, rather than the relative interest, paid. This explains why they still borrow from finance houses (who charge up to double or more the interest charged by clearing banks) even though, to the enduring amazement and satisfaction of the finance houses' marketing managers, their poorest customers commonly know that cheaper credit is available elsewhere (for instance, in proper clearing banks). Another explanation is that the alternative sources of credit may be unapproachable, or may simply not serve them.[2]

It is not yet obvious what will replace the system of bank current account charges, although the banks are very conscious of the need to have some mechanism 'to drive away down-market customers'.[3] In future, this will probably be a system of screening, with customers allocated to categories qualifying for different ranges of services. The screening will probably be done on a points system. The customer or the bank clerk will fill in a form with the customer's personal details. Points will be given for such indicators of personal affluence as a high income, home-ownership (perhaps even the area in which the home is!), length of employment and so on. Customers obtaining full points would qualify for the full range of services. Customers with a low points score would get restricted services, for example they would be refused a cheque guarantee card, which would then effectively limit them to cash withdrawals at the bank where their account is, and make their cheques unacceptable in shops.

The points system is already widely in use among finance houses as a way of determining the maximum amounts that can be lent to customers with minimal risk of default. Here it is widely considered to be 'scientific' because there is a logical relationship between income and wealth, and the amount of credit which their owner can comfortably service. However, there is not such a clear or logical link between these factors, and a person's ability to make prudent use of particular current account facilities. An alternative selection criterion could be by simple categories of size of income, or source of income. The latter, in particular, could be used to exclude social security claimants and state pensioners, whose low-balance accounts are especially unwanted by the banks.

Life assurance

Among all classes of society, life assurance plays an important role: for the rich, as a tax-efficient savings medium; for the poor, as a supplement to a mean and gapped welfare state, to secure house-hold finance against the demise of a main income-earner and provide basic financial reserves. Life assurance is the purchase of a guaranteed sum of money payable on the death of the person assured or on the expiry of a fixed term of ten years or more. Premiums are paid for this service, out of which expenses and commission are deducted before they are invested to provide the guaranteed sum (nowadays usually with additional profits) and make it greater than the total premiums paid.

In the life assurance business, there is an essential class distinction between the two branches of this service: ordinary life assurance, and industrial or home service insurance. The difference between the two is in the mode of delivery of the service. In the ordinary branch, the premium is delivered by the customer to the life assurance company's office or its broker. With industrial life assurance, premiums are collected from the home by a representative of the firm. In 1984, over £1.2 billion was collected from over 10 million homes of the housebound and the less financially aware in the United Kingdom. Despite the public image of friendly and personal service promoted by the industrial life offices, this type of insurance ensures that the least well-off get the worst value for their premiums.

The reason for this is that the industrial policy-holder pays nearly twice as much in commission and management expenses (which are deducted before the premiums are invested) as the ordinary policy-holder. In 1984, management expenses and commission took up 38.9% of industrial insurance premium income. For ordinary life business, this percentage was 21.7% in 1984.[4] Many industrial policy-holders find that, if forced by circumstances to surrender their policy, they get nothing, or a relatively trivial sum back, even after paying premiums for years. Had they an ordinary policy, they would certainly have received more. And even if they pay to maturity, the higher cost of collecting their premiums ensures that they get, for each pound of their premium, much less than the ordinary policy-holder. Professor L C B Gower, in his *Review of Investor Protection*, cites information from an insurance intermediary that ordinary benefits can be as much as 50% better than those of industrial policies, although the Industrial Life Offices Association told him that the difference on ten- to twenty-year endowment policies is 'typically in the range 5 per cent to 20 per cent'.[5]

With increasing financial awareness, the number of industrial policies has declined, from 87.8m in 1975 to 66.3m at the end of 1984. This decline has been inhibited by the obvious difficulty of breaking off from such a mode of arranging insurance payments and the difficulty of switching over to ordinary insurance. At the end of 1984, there were, by contrast, only 29.3m ordinary policies. The average value of the latter, in terms of sums assured and bonuses, was £8,976. The average industrial policy was worth a mere fraction of that — £323. This is partly because of the rudimentary nature of these policies and the way in which they are marketed, so that sums assured can only be increased by taking out additional policies.[6]

The average industrial policy-holder is also poorer and of lower social status than the average ordinary life assured. As Table 5 shows, in general, industrial life assurance is used by considerably less than half the number of adults that have ordinary life assurance. The holding of ordinary life assurance is most common in social class C2 (where households are headed by a skilled manual worker), 47.3% of whose adults have ordinary life assurance policies. Industrial life assurance is most common in social class D (ie, among semi-skilled and unskilled manual workers and their families), 22.1% of whose adults have this kind of policy.

The differences of income between holders of these two types of insurance is even greater. Ordinary life assurance is most popular among adults with an income of between £11,000 and £15,000, over half of whom have this kind of life assurance. By contrast, industrial life assurance is most common among adults with incomes around half of that (£5,000-£6,999), nearly a quarter of whom use this kind of insurance.

Table 5: *Life assurance policy-holders (%)*

	Those with a current death or maturity policy	Those contributing to an industrial policy
All adults	41.9	16.9
Men	48.9	16.6
Women	35.8	17.2
Social class:		
AB	43.7	7.0
C1	44.8	14.9
C2	47.3	22.0
D	41.7	22.1
E	24.4	14.7
Income group:		
Income not stated	21.9	10.3
£2,999 or less	25.3	14.4
£3,000 to £4,999	35.2	20.3
£5,000 to £6,999	47.8	24.2
£7,000 to £8,999	53.2	22.9
£9,000 to £10,999	56.2	21.2
£11,000 to £14,999	57.7	16.9
£15,000 and over	55.0	11.8

Source: Target Index Group, BRMB © 1985

Thus, the savings of the better-off are multiplied by the best efforts of the insurance companies in competition for up-market business, while the savings of the less well-off are merely increased in a rather pedestrian way by this segmentation of the life assurance business. When the various tax privileges of insurance and pension funds are included in the calculation, this regressive effect is enhanced. This could be one reason for welcoming the abolition in 1984 of income tax relief on life assurance premiums, even though the reform hit the poor, who need this relief most, as well as the rich, who made most use of it.

Technological change, competition and public policy

The view that was presented above is necessarily a very selective one that would give a false impression if some comment was not made about the changes, some of which are quite radical, that are now taking place. Their eventual results can only be sketchily predicted with any degree of accuracy, even by those most intimately concerned with promoting these changes. Broadly speaking, there are two general and overlapping categories of factors determining these developments: technological change and institutional reform.

The general effect of technological change has been to make more feasible, economically viable and accessible a wide range of existing as well as new financial services. However, this is unlikely to bring much benefit to those presently unbanked (see Table 4 above). This is for three reasons. First of all, many of the new services, such as the electronic transfer of funds in shops, presuppose the possession of a bank account by their user. This is because they still require some settlements between banking accounts.

Second, many of these services, such as electronic home banking, require a sizeable payment into the new account, plus substantial additional fees for individual transactions — for example, the Nottingham Building Society/Bank of Scotland's home banking scheme requires the payment into the new account of £500. To these costs must be added those of purchasing the computer hardware, VDUs and software, as Graham Murdock's chapter in this pamphlet explains.

Third, most of them require considerable dedication to financial dealing and technological gadgetry. This is not characteristic of most people, let alone the unbanked, while the latter can least afford to hire or purchase the necessary advice and expertise. Hence the greatest appeal of these services to the young and well-educated minority of the population, rather than the elderly, the poor and the educationally deprived. There is also an irony in the fact that for the really rich, the trend in financial service development is not so much towards greater mechanisation, but towards the more personal service across a wider range of activities that is known as 'priority' or private banking.

One can tentatively predict that one effect of technological change will be to polarise even further (at least in the near future) the differences in the type and quality of financial services available to the rich and the poor. To the existing segmentation along the dimensions of wealth and income will be added segmentation along the dimensions of financial and technological aptitude. As the services offered change rapidly in quality and kind, considerable acumen will be necessary to obtain the most advantageous and suitable service. The wealthy, whatever their personal financial ineptitude, will be able to buy appropriate advice. Clinging to 'safe' and familiar services, the less well-off will probably end up with less beneficial and obsolete services, and thus have their financial disadvantages compounded.

The second category of factors determining developments in financial services is that of institutional change. In this respect, the government and the financial institutions all seem to be in agreement that the best way to improve financial services is by encouraging greater competition between different kinds of firms. This will ostensibly drive out of the market those who give an inferior service, or force them to correct their ways, while ease of entry into markets is supposed to ensure a steady flow of improving innovation. Competition has been regarded as a potent nostrum in the financial establishment since the Bank of England's Competition and Credit Control Policy, introduced in 1971. It has been embraced by even such potential critics as the Wilson Committee on the Functioning of Financial Institutions and the National Consumer Council.[7] To its credit, competition has achieved some positive successes, such as the abolition of bank charges and the limited opening of banks on Saturdays.

However, greater competition alone will be of little help to the least well-off, and may even be of detriment to them. This is because greater competition between building societies, banks, finance houses and so on is making them much more commercially orientated. Seeking new customers much more actively than in the past, they have been seeking them among the better-off, rather than the unbanked poor, since by definition the latter have less money.

Thus, even where there is serious competition for the accounts of the low paid, it is among students who are expected to be well paid in the future. No one wants the humble accounts of social classes D and E, and certainly not those of the bulk of the retired population, who have no hope of ever becoming rich. The clearing banks' 'free banking' marketing strategy is aimed at the already banked social and income groups — even persuading people in them to open additional accounts. New customers are carefully vetted to limit the influx of 'down-market' accounts.

Competition and greater commercialisation among financial firms is not only unlikely to end their neglect of the poor. It may also be to the latter's disadvantage. In the past, there have been financial institutions that have specifically catered for the financial needs of the less well-off, most notably the Trustee Savings Banks. These were established in the nineteenth century, in the spirit of Victorian self-improvement, to encourage saving among the poor. In promoting competition and a stronger commercial ethos, the government has amalgamated the Trustee Savings Banks into one bank, which is to issue shares on the Stock Exchange and become a joint stock bank. As a consequence of this, the Trustee Savings Bank is now firmly set to compete for middle-class business. The general manager of the TSB's finance house subsidiary, the United

Dominion Trust, has singled out for development 'the fast-growing markets, which he identified as finance for the home-owning and professional classes'.[8] This move towards a better-heeled clientele is a notable feature of the TSB's 'privatisation' strategy.

This tendency to go up-market is not really surprising: that is where the money is, and mutual and public sector institutions, such as building societies and the Trustee Savings Banks, when forced to compete with commercial financial firms, must inevitably gravitate towards these markets.

The other institutional changes are the pressures to force the poor and financially unsophisticated into the mainstream banking and financial system. Most obvious is the government's policy of moving towards the repeal of the Truck Acts, so that all wages can be paid by credit transfers to bank accounts. This would effectively force unbanked workers into the banking system. It is a crucial issue for the poor since, as we have seen, the banks on the whole neither want their custom nor are prepared to offer appropriate and economic services.[9] More controversial is the government's policy of limiting the scope of the state earnings-related pension scheme (SERPS), and encouraging more private and company pension schemes funded through commercial investment institutions.

Then there is the pervasive, informal, but much more insidious, pressure on the unbanked to enter the banking system in order to have convenient access to income and make payments more easily. This compulsion is increasing as the unbanked are reduced to a smaller minority outside the normal income and payment distributing mechanism of our society. Furthermore, certain legislative changes have added to this pressure in indirect ways. For example, the 1975 Social Security Pensions Act allows firms to opt out of the state pensions system if they can provide a scheme that is at least as good. In recent years, the first pensioners have started drawing on these schemes. But before they can receive any benefits from them, they are usually asked to supply details of the clearing bank account into which their pension will be paid. This is forcing many pensioners to open accounts. Other pressures are the introduction of charges by the post office for the payment of, for example, electricity bills across its counters, and the promotion of social security payments by means of bank credits.

While recent changes have made financial firms concentrate their efforts on up-market clients, or at least the middle classes, the poor and low paid are being forced to use expensive (even if the high cost is not visible, as in industrial life assurance) and inappropriate (such as banking, where an ethos of service to the landed and commercial upper classes still predominates) services. This belies the comfortable view of many financial managers, bankers and their government supervisors, according to which the 'market' for financial services is so segmented, and financial firms are so enterprising, that all sections of the population receive the financial services appropriate to their needs and abilities. At the top of the market, 'priority banking' provides the widest range of services for 'high net worth individuals' (ie, the rich, generally defined as having assets of £250,000 and more). Below that, the mainstream clearing banks provide banking services for the middle and professional classes. Finance houses, the smaller clearing banks (the Yorkshire, Co-operative and Trustee Savings Banks), and building societies provide rather more rudimentary services for the clerical and better-off manual workers, who find the august atmosphere in the halls of the major clearing banks uncongenial. Below them are the unbanked, for whom industrial insurance and check-trading companies provide very primitive payments and savings services. At different levels, mutual associations, such as investment clubs and credit unions, also operate.

This stratified financial system is not only being compressed, as the unbanked are forced into the banked sectors and financial firms move up-market, but it is also intrinsically unfair and regressive. The poor not only get worse, if any, service but they also pay more for it in terms of higher charges and lower returns on their savings. Yet financial services are becoming less equitable as it becomes more difficult to manage one's financial affairs, draw income and make payments, without them.

Ultimately, a financial system which inhibits the social and economic activity of the least well-off, which gives them inferior services and concentrates every conscious effort on satisfying the financial needs and whims of those engaged in upward economic and social mobility, is a social arrangement for the redistribution of wealth and income from those that have less to those that have more. Therefore, it deserves as much attention and criticism as government policy on the distribution of income and wealth. Moreover, as long as income payments and savings are processed through a financial system that curbs the self-improvement of the poor, and accelerates the decline of the near poor into absolute poverty, by overcharging them and devaluing their savings, a fundamental reform of financial institutions is essential to deal effectively with the problem of poverty.

Notes and references

1 *Banking Services and the Consumer: a report by the National Consumer Council*, Methuen, 1983.
2 The exploitation of the poor by some of the finance houses is one of the more profitable but degrading activities of our financial system. It surfaces rarely in the media in scandals such as that surrounding Hodge & Co in the mid-1970s. Much should be written about this, but regrettably too little systematic information is available.

3 This was stated to be a function of bank charges in P Frazer and D Vittas, *The Retail Banking Revolution*, Michael Lafferty Publications, 1982, p xxiii.

4 These statistics are drawn from *Life Assurance in the United Kingdom 1980-1984*, Association of British Insurers, 1985.

5 L C B Gower, *Review of Investor Protection: Report Part I*, HMSO, 1984, p 190. See also A Masey, 'Savings, insurance and credit' in Frances Williams (ed), *Why the Poor Pay More*, Macmillan/NCC, 1977, and in Counter Information Services, *Your Money and Your Life: insurance companies and pension funds*, 1974.

6 See note 4 above.

7 National Consumer Council, note 1 above, and *Committee to Review the Functioning of Financial Institutions: Report*, HMSO, 1982.

8 *Financial Times*, 8 March 1985.

9 D Byrne, *Low Pay Check: reforming the Truck Acts*, Low Pay Unit, 1983.

6 Poor connections: income inequality and the 'information society'

GRAHAM MURDOCK

We are constantly being told by politicians and pundits of all persuasions that Britain is becoming an 'information society' in which information of all kinds will be more abundant and available than ever before. Developments in technology are presented as the keys that will make it possible for everyone to obtain the information they need at a stroke. With suitable additions and modifications, so we are told, the domestic telephone and television set will provide access to an unparalleled range of services. This is an attractive vision, but it conveniently forgets the general economic context within which these developments are taking place.

In line with the government's declared aims of rolling back the boundaries of the state and of reviving the enterprise economy, virtually all of the new information industries have been launched as commercial ventures. Most require customers to pay for the services they use, as well as for the extra equipment needed to obtain them. At the same time, cuts in funding for organisations in the public and voluntary sectors are reducing access to free information provision. As a result, the poor stand to be excluded from the emerging 'information society' twice over. They are priced out of the markets for the new commercial information services and left with an impoverished and overstretched system of public provision which is increasingly unable to meet either their demands or their needs. We can see this pincer movement working very clearly if we look at recent developments in telecommunications. What is happening in this area is particularly important since the telephone network is a major point of connection to information services, both old and new.

Trying to disconnect you: the telephone system

The telephone system provides an essential link to key information and support services at several levels. First, it is the quickest and easiest way of contacting emergency services. These include not only the basic police, fire and medical services, but also the crisis counselling and advice offered by agencies such as the Samaritans and Rape Crisis Centres. Second, as the *Yellow Pages* slogan puts it, a telephone lets your fingers do the walking, providing convenient access to practical information on opening hours, bus and train timetables, the price and availability of goods, and a range of other things. Third, it extends the informal networks of support, advice and information offered by friends, relatives and neighbours. This is particularly important for people living alone and those whose physical mobility is restricted by disability or lack of money. And lastly, a phone often provides the most convenient point of access to the free professional expertise provided by Citizens' Advice Bureaux (CABx), law centres, welfare rights centres and consumer advice centres. A recent survey of CABx in London found that telephone calls accounted for a third of all the requests dealt with and almost a half (46.8%) of the consumer enquiries.[1] Similarly, the rapid rise in the ratio of claimants to DHSS staff and the fall-off in home-visiting since 1981 have led to a marked increase in telephone enquiries to social security offices.[2] The staff cuts and other major changes proposed in the 1986 Social Security Bill will undoubtedly reinforce claimants' need for telephone services still further.

These instances illustrate a more general trend. Advice and information services have been under tremendous pressure in recent years as rising unemployment and social security dependence have increased the numbers of people in need of help and the range of problems they are confronted with. At the same time, funding for these services, especially those like law centres which are used heavily by poorer clients, has been depressed by the mounting financial and political pressures on local authority spending.[3] As a result, centres are being forced to close, making physical access to essential sources of advice more difficult and time-consuming. According to one recent estimate, 85 out of the 159 independent advice centres in London were under threat with the abolishing of the Greater London Council, while others around the country face threats to their funding because of ratecapping and cuts in urban aid.[4]

In this situation, possessing a telephone or having one within easy reach becomes even more important as a source of access to advice. However, the figures for telephone possession clearly show that low income households are the least likely to have one. According to the latest Family Expenditure Survey, although over three-quarters (78%) of all households in the country had a phone in 1984, 47% of low income single pensioners and 40% of single parent households with one child still had to rely on public call boxes or other people's telephones.[5] Current policies in the field of telecommunications do nothing to improve this situation. On the contrary, they are likely to exacerbate it and to disconnect even more poor households from easy access to the telephone network.

Over the last five years, British Telecom (BT) has changed from a public utility to a commercially-minded corporation seeking to maximise its profits in the emerging information marketplace. There are two basic aspects to this shift:

Liberalisation: the ending of BT's historic monopoly over the supply of telephone services and the introduction of limited competition in the form of Cable and Wireless's Mercury network.

Denationalisation: moving BT from the public to the market sector by selling a majority share stake of 50.2% to private investors in November 1984.

These developments have already had a significant effect on the amount that ordinary domestic customers have to pay for their telephone services, and they are likely to push up prices still further in future.

As a public utility, BT aimed to bring telephone services within the reach of everyone by maintaining a nationwide network of public call boxes and pricing local calls (which make up the bulk of most people's telephone usage) at less than their economic cost. Historically, the losses on these services were subsidised out of the profits from long distance and international calls, most of which are made by business users. But as the expense of maintaining and modernising the telephone network escalated, pressures mounted for local calls to cover more of their costs, while business users pushed for cheaper services. The Post Office, as it then was, responded and, while the real price of local calls at peak times rose by 183% between 1973 and 1978, the price of trunk calls over thirty-five miles or more actually dropped by 13%.[6] Liberalisation has intensified this trend and led to tariffs being re-balanced even more firmly in favour of business customers.

Mercury was granted a licence to compete with BT in February 1982. The company's aim was to cream off a proportion of BT's lucrative business traffic by providing an advanced fibre optic trunk network linking the country's major commercial centres. BT responded swiftly by slashing prices on the routes most heavily used by business customers in order to steal a march on Mercury before their system was up and running. Charges on the hundred major trunk routes were cut by 35% and the price of transatlantic calls significantly reduced. In 1980 it cost £2.26 to make a three-minute call across the Atlantic (in 1983 prices); in 1983 it only cost £1.65. A survey comparing telephone charges in a number of industrial countries at the end of that year concluded that 'British telecommunications pricing is clearly biased to favour services used by business. Telex charges are at bargain basement level and so are long distance telephone calls . . . but local calls are far costlier in Britain than elsewhere.'[7] These differentials have been further reinforced by the effects of privatisation.

As a commercial corporation BT's primary aim is to maximise the returns from its existing activities and to develop new profit centres. Since analysts are generally agreed that business services are likely to generate the bulk of BT's revenue growth over the next few years, there is even more incentive to reduce charges for services which are most exposed to competition and to get domestic users to pay a greater proportion of the costs of providing local services. However, BT cannot charge consumers whatever it likes. The current agreement commits it to a formula which limits annual increases in the 'basket' of charges covering line rentals and dialled calls within the UK to three percentage points below the general rate of inflation as measured by the retail price index. This RPI-3 formula (as it's known) only applies to the 'basket' as a whole, however. Within this limit, charges for specific items can be increased by considerably more, as the last round of price rises at the end of 1985 clearly demonstrated.

These were based on an RPI figure of 7%, which meant that BT could only raise charges in the agreed 'basket' by a maximum of 4% overall. In the event, they opted to limit themselves to 3.7% and to add the unused 0.3% to their 1986 allowance. However, concealed within this relatively modest total figure were rises for some domestic charges which were actually above the agreed rate of inflation. Quarterly rentals rose by 8.6% to £16.45, the maximum charge for an exchange line connection rose by 11.7% to £85, while existing customers taking over a line when they moved house were faced with an entirely new charge of £10. As a result of these increases, anyone wanting to be connected to the telephone system for the first time could be faced with a bill for over a hundred pounds in connection and rental charges before they had made any calls at all. Moreover, under the supplementary benefits single payments regulations, installation and rental of a telephone are expressly exempt from the list of items for which claimants may receive help from the Department of Health and Social Security, and it is only in exceptional circumstances that local authority social services departments make a grant under the Chronically Sick and Disabled Persons Act.

Soon after the last round of price rises were announced in October 1985, the Office of Telecommunications (Oftel), which is responsible for regulating the system, published details of the final arrangements for connecting Mercury's trunk system to BT's local and international networks. These have been designed to promote a comprehensive alternative for business users by ensuring that Mercury's customers will be able to call any destination in the UK and abroad via BT's lines, and are widely regarded as highly favourable to Mercury. In response, BT warned that a further re-balancing of tariffs between long distance and local calls was inevitable if the profitability of its UK network was to be maintained, adding that 'residential and small business customers are likely to end up paying more, sooner, to offset the benefits to large business customers from Mercury's arrival'.[8] Exactly how much 'more' this will be remains to be seen, but there is little doubt that the least well-off will be the biggest losers. Nor will public call boxes provide an adequate safety net for those unable to afford a domestic phone.

Compared to a number of other advanced industrial countries, Britain has never had a particularly extensive system of public payphones. At the beginning of 1985, there were 293,500 installed in shops, pubs and blocks of flats, but only 76,500 in openly public locations — 2,300 less than New York City and well under half the number in France (170,000). There are no plans to expand the present network. Indeed, some call boxes are likely to disappear. Under the terms of its operating licence, BT is entitled to close any call box with takings of less than £185 a year. There are presently some 10,000 in this category, though the fact that closures (particularly in rural areas) attract a good deal of political attention and adverse publicity is likely to keep BT's closure programme to fairly modest proportions, at least for the moment. More immediately significant are BT's plans to modernise the payphone network and convert the substantial losses it now makes into profits by 1990. These moves are likely to make an important impact on the poorest users' access to telephone services.

Over the next ten years, BT will replace the familiar red boxes with American-style open kiosks made of aluminium and steel. These are harder to vandalise, so fewer will be 'out of order' at any one time, and the absence of a heavy door will make them easier for the elderly and disabled to use. At the same time, over 10% of the new payphones will require the caller to have a fixed denomination card which has to be bought in advance. Others will take credit cards. This expansion of cashless call boxes will cut BT's costs by reducing the number of coin boxes that can be broken into, and it will be more convenient for those who can afford to buy their calls in advance. But for those who can't and who are outside of the credit card system, it will restrict access to the telephone system still further. They will also be hit by the sharp increases in call prices which are necessary to move the payphone system into profit. Unlike the price of calls made on a domestic phone, call box charges fall outside the RPI-3 agreement and can be raised by whatever BT thinks the market will bear. This has already led to rises of as much as 100% on some services during

BT's first year of operation as a private corporation, and increases well above the general rate of inflation seem likely in future.

Locked out from logging on: value-added services

Lack of access to a telephone also excludes people from the growing range of value-added services which are provided and paid for on top of the basic telephone network. The best established of these is BT's Prestel service which allows people to call up pages of information from a central computer store, for display on a purpose-built monitor or on a television set which has been adapted for the purpose. When Prestel was first introduced in the autumn of 1979, it was viewed as an attractive new public utility which would have some three million subscribers by 1983. However, by the end of 1982 only 23,086 terminals had been installed and only 14% of those were in residential households. The main reason for this sluggish take-up was the high costs involved in using the system. This is still the case. In addition to having a telephone and paying local call charges for the time they are on the system, Prestel users have to adapt their television set at a cost of £100 upwards, pay a yearly subscription of £26, pay 6p per minute for the time they are connected to the central computer on Saturday mornings or during business hours on weekdays (though all other times are free), and pay some of the information-providers for each page of material they call up.

These charges put Prestel well beyond the means of low income families and ensure that the information it provides continues to reflect the requirements of the business users and affluent households who are its major customers. In order to change this situation and realise the system's considerable potential as a public information resource, two conditions would have to be met. An extensive network of terminals which could be used for minimal or zero costs would have to be installed in libraries and other public locations, and the information available would have to be extended to meet a broader range of local and social needs.

Unfortunately, substantial developments along these lines are highly unlikely in the present climate. In a situation where the squeeze on public funding is already making it impossible for many libraries to sustain their established services at a level sufficient to meet public demand, few are in a position to add a comprehensive network of computer-based services. Financial restrictions also make it more or less impossible for most voluntary sector organisations to contemplate setting up and maintaining the kind of data bases that are needed. At the same time, public sector organisations are increasingly affected by the drive to develop a strong 'tradeable information' industry based on customer payments for the material they consume. As a report by the influential Information Techno-logy Advisory Panel has argued, this goal can only be realised if the amount of information which is freely available in other forms is reduced. As they point out:

> much information at present comes free, or apparently free, and a small charge is sufficient to deter users. The charging structure of Prestel made access to railway timetables appear expensive by comparison with looking at a printed timetable or telephon-ing a station... [similarly] the provision by government of a free publication on a particular subject could render unviable a commercial service which is charging for the same information.[9]

The solution, as they see it, is simplicity itself. Transfer informa-tion from the public sector to the marketplace and charge for access to it. If this principle gains ground, the poor will be doubly disadvantaged within the information system: excluded from the new computer-based systems by the high price of entry, and left with an impoverished and restricted system of public provision.

Exclusion from Prestel doesn't only affect access to information, however. It also limits access to the additional services that are being developed to encourage more domestic customers to sub-scribe to the system. One of the most interesting from the point of view of its potential for meeting social needs is home shopping. Though, here again, as with the basic information services, it is the more affluent households who are the major target. The recently announced Telecard Supershop scheme typifies the emerging trend. This allows Prestel subscribers in certain areas of London to use their terminals to order goods from a list of over 3,500 items and to have them delivered to the door by van the same day or the next day at the latest. The only additional payment required is the cost of the phone calls used to place the order. Such a system would be of considerable benefit to people with mobility problems, but the scheme is designed to make profits not to meet social needs. Consequently, it is confined to the richer boroughs, such as Westminster, Kensington and Chelsea and Camden, where house-holds spend around £75 a week on food and drink, compared with the average of £46 for London as a whole.

The more ambitious Homelink scheme also operates to exclude the poor. This is a joint venture between BT, the Nottingham Building Society, the Bank of Scotland and a number of retailers. It offers home shopping and banking facilities on a nationwide basis plus access to Prestel's basic information services. Subscribers joining the Prestel system for the first time can avoid the full costs of connection by renting the extra equipment they need from Homelink for £51 a year plus VAT. They have to pay the normal Prestel charges on top, but once on the system they can order goods and take advantage of a variety of special offers relatively cheaply. In order to remain on the system, however, customers have to keep a minimum of £250 in a Nottingham Building Society account. If their balance drops below this figure, they are disconnected. Since most poor households cannot possibly meet this condition, they are excluded from the scheme's considerable benefits.

Not having a car, coupled with the difficulty and expense of making long journeys by public transport, already excludes poor households from the choice and cost advantages of shopping at the hypermarkets on the edge of towns, and to a lesser extent at city centre chain stores and supermarkets, and obliges them to rely on the shops in their local area, which generally carry fewer brands and charge higher prices. By adding to the advantages already enjoyed by better-off households, commercially oriented home shopping systems compound the problems facing the poor. Yet the technology could be mobilised to serve their needs, as the experimental service in Gateshead clearly shows. This has been using telephone links to Prestel terminals in the local social security headquarters, together with publicly accessible terminals in libraries and sheltered accommodation and terminals in the homes of those most in need, to bring the benefits of home shopping to a range of groups who would otherwise be excluded. They include the elderly, the disabled and the 25% of the local population who cannot afford to travel into the city centre on a regular basis. However, this has only been possible because of extensive subsidies from public and corporate sources. Despite its success in meeting social needs, initiatives like this are unlikely to be repeated in many other places in the foreseeable future, given the increasing pressure on public funding.

Far from expanding the poor's access to information, then, present government policies offer them the worst of both worlds. Excluded from the new commercially oriented telecommunications services, they are left with a system of public provision which is being whittled away. We find the same basic combination when we look at what is happening to the other major source of most people's information -- television.

Screened out: the new television industries

The domestic television screen already plays a central role in British social and cultural life. Virtually every household, even the poorest, has at least one set, and in the average home this will be on for between 4½ and 5½ hours a day (depending on the time of year), with the average individual over 4 years old watching broadcast programmes for around three hours. However, the poor and the unemployed often watch for longer, since, as Alan Tomlinson points out in his chapter, lack of money effectively excludes them from a wide range of alternative leisure options. For most people, television will be their major source of information about what is happening outside their local area, and their main point of access to the arguments and explanations that put events in context, connect them to everyday experience, and explore the possibilities for change. Consequently, television's ability to address the full range of relevant issues and opinions and to provide information, analysis and commentary in depth, plays a crucial role in helping people to understand their situation, recognise their rights and formulate options for practical action.

Up until recently, television was synonymous with broadcasting, in the sense that everything that appeared on the small screen was produced or purchased by either the BBC or the ITV companies. This is no longer the case. Alongside the expansion of broadcast services with the introduction of breakfast time television and the launching of Channel Four, recent years have seen the emergence of new television industries which are using the developing technologies of video, cable and satellite distribution to provide additional options for viewing. Enthusiasts of these developments argue that they will extend the overall diversity of provision and open up an unparalleled range of choices for consumers. This is an enticing vision, but it conveniently ignores several pertinent points.

In the first place, choice within this new system is not free. It is expensive and, as we shall see, the current entry charges are well beyond the means of most low-income households. Second, multiplicity is not the same thing as diversity. It is possible to increase substantially the number of television channels without extending the range of information on offer. And third, even a modest growth in the new television industries is likely to have a significant impact on basic broadcast services, forcing them to cut costs and compete more aggressively for viewers by offering more popular entertainment. This, in turn, puts pressure on the budgets for factual programming, forcing cut-backs and reducing the range and depth of information available to the ordinary licence payer. Although these dynamics are still in the process of developing, the present situation of cable television provides clear confirmation of points one and two.

Many commentators have assumed that because operators are awarded franchises for particular areas, cable will make a valuable addition to local information networks. This view is based on a misconception. Although the technology can be used to deliver local television news, supply local information and provide opportunities for community groups to make programmes putting over their point of view, the core business of cable is selling the entertainment channels packaged by the major national and international suppliers. These are of two kinds: advertising supported services which are sold to subscribers as part of a basic package of services, and premium channels which require an additional payment. The basic channels which are currently available in Britain include Screensport, Music Box (which is built around rock videos), the Children's Channel, Lifestyle (a television women's magazine), and the general entertainment service, Sky Channel. Both the major premium services — Premiere and Mirror-Vision — offer recent feature films. Access to these services is relatively expensive, however.

If we take the cost of the licence and the fee for renting a modest 14″ set, it currently costs a minimum of £10.78 a month to receive basic broadcast services in colour. A 16″ set pushes this figure up to £15.78, without including the hidden costs of watching ITV in the form of higher prices for heavily advertised goods. According to recent estimates, these can add anything between 1p and 3p to the cost of each viewing hour.[10] Subscribing to the full range of cable services requires a household to more than double this basic expenditure on television. To obtain the full service offered by Greenwich Cablescene, for example, costs £21.65 a month, though subscribers who don't want or can't afford the premium channels can get a package of basic services for £8. Croydon Cable, launched in September 1985, is even more expensive, at £23 a month for all channels, and Clyde Cable in Glasgow, launched a month later, more expensive still, at £30.33 a month for the full service and £16.25 for the basic package.

The operators recognise that prices like these put cable beyond the reach of households on low incomes and they are now concentrating their attention on more affluent households, who have the additional benefit of being attractive to the advertisers who support the basic services. At the beginning of 1986, for example, Robert Maxwell, who owns the old Rediffusion cable network, the country's largest, announced that he was cutting his staff by almost 400, and suspending active selling in twenty-four out of the forty areas covered, in order to concentrate on the sixteen locations with the best growth potential. The selected areas, which included Bristol, Hastings, Oxford and Reading, were almost all in the relatively affluent areas of the South and Midlands, while the others were mostly located in depressed northern locations such as Hartlepool and Tyneside. This geographic bias is further reinforced by the franchising arrangements for new systems, which allow prospective operators to select the areas they wish to bid for.

Recent trade surveys suggest that the arrival of these new systems, coupled with the more targeted approach to marketing in the older systems and the high rate of disconnection in poorer areas, is increasing the proportion of better-off households among cable subscribers. Even so, the cable industry is not in a particularly buoyant state. Although the number of homes 'passed' by cable (and therefore capable of being connected up) has risen during the last twelve months, the number actually subscribing has fallen, placing a number of operators in financial difficulties. In response, they have looked for ways of cutting their costs, and local services have been the first to suffer. In August 1985, Greenwich Cable-scene, one of the pioneers of community programming, halved its staff and discontinued local television production. A few months later, Aberdeen Cable followed suit by closing its local news operation, and in February 1986, Swindon Cable shut down its showpiece production department and cancelled its thrice weekly local news magazine. As managing director Tim Smith put it: 'Our business is in cable ... we do not believe we should be involved in television production.' In other words, cable is about selling professionally packaged entertainment. Local information and programming is a marginal extra, useful for public relations but dispensable.

In future, only the more affluent groups of subscribers are likely to be provided with information services tailored to their needs. For example, for an additional monthly charge on top of the £23.50 subscription for the full package of basic and premium channels, Arab-speaking users of Westminster Cable can now receive 8-10 hours of Arabic programming a day, beamed by satellite from Dubai. In contrast, cable services are unlikely to add much extra to the information and analysis available to basic subscribers, with the possible exception of teletext services with a local component.

Without a significant change in present policies towards cable, this trend is unlikely to be reversed in future for two reasons. First, under the current rules for granting franchises, the provision of local services is optional rather than compulsory, and the Cable Authority has made no secret of the fact that it sees its first duty as helping a fledgling industry to develop with the minimum of restrictions. Second, cable is about to face a challenge to its core business of selling additional entertainment channels from Direct Broadcasting Satellite systems (DBS). The cable channels available in Britain are already distributed by satellite, but at the moment the signals are collected by the cable operators and relayed to subscribers over local cable systems. DBS enables consumers to cut out the cable operator and receive signals directly, using a small dish antenna.

At the moment, satellite dishes are very much a luxury commodity. NEC are currently selling one for £1,460, though if you live in one of the areas served by DER's pilot rental experiment, you can hire one for £50 a month plus a further £12 for the right to watch the programmes. As DER's Head of Technical Services noted when the scheme was launched, it is only 'likely to appeal to people with higher than normal incomes'.[11] However, as new DBS services come on stream over the next two or three years, making mass dish production feasible, prices are likely to drop considerably. British Aerospace has already designed a dish small enough to stand on a windowsill or on top of a normal television set which it claims will cost around £200 to buy or £20 a month to rent, though consumers would still have to subscribe to premium services on top of that. Even at these prices, however, satellite dishes are unlikely to become a standard fixture in many low income households. But even if the market is confined to the more affluent half of the population, competition from DBS, coupled with other pressures, could still have a substantial effect on the range and depth of the informational programming provided by the basic broadcasting services. Indeed, the dynamics involved are already evident.

Although cable currently reaches only a small proportion of homes with television, the services it offers are relatively popular and occupy 21% of total weekly viewing time in the households which subscribe. In an average week, the most popular service, Sky Channel, is seen by more viewers in cable homes than either BBC2 or Channel Four.[12] This small but significant inroad into their share of the television audience adds to the problems that public broadcasters already face from rising production costs, and, in the BBC's case, from a licence fee award that falls some way short of the level needed to maintain activities at their current level. In this situation informational programmes, and especially the features, documentaries and community programmes needed to sustain a diversity of analysis and comment, are particularly vulnerable. They can be expensive to make, they don't usually attract high ratings, and they are increasingly likely to be criticised and attacked by corporations, state agencies and members of the government. Faced with this combination of political and financial pressures, public broadcasters have several options, all of which have implications for the range and depth of information provision.

In the first place, they can cut back on informational programming and compete more aggressively for viewers by concentrating on popular entertainment. The cut of £1.3m in the current budget for information programmes recently announced by the BBC, coupled with the increase in game shows and chat shows, is a step in this direction. Second, they can reduce programme-making costs by seeking co-production arrangements with outside organisations. This is a highly attractive option financially, but it carries certain cultural costs. The fact that co-productions have to be acceptable and intelligible in the markets served by all the partners to the deal may restrict the range of themes and issues that can be dealt with. It works against topics which are judged too controversial or parochial and favours subject matter that is safe and saleable. This means more productions dealing with historical themes, the natural world and the arts, rather than investigative features which probe the institutions with significant power over people's lives or access programmes which offer a platform for the social policy concerns of citizens' groups.

Third, public broadcasters can respond to the competition of the new television industries by entering the emerging marketplace on their own account and selling their programmes to cable and satellite operators. The Superchannel project recently launched by a consortium of leading ITV companies is a significant move in this direction. It aims to use a satellite link to beam British-made programmes to the rapidly expanding cable networks of Continental Europe. Supporters of this option argue that it is a valuable way of raising extra revenue which can be ploughed back into original production and used to cross-subsidise riskier and less popular programmes. On the other hand, if income from these secondary markets becomes an essential part of broadcast finances, which is quite likely in the present situation, there is a distinct possibility that the sales tail will end up wagging the production dog and that possible projects will come to be evaluated more for their sales potential than for their ability to meet the information needs of domestic licence payers who can only afford basic broadcast services.

It is too early to say how these trends will affect information provision in the longer term. The structure of the broadcasting and television industries is changing very rapidly at the present time, as new entrants jostle for position and established institutions look for ways of adapting to the new, more competitive environments. The current debate over whether or not the BBC should take advertising adds a further note of uncertainty. Nevertheless, beneath the appearance of constant movement it is already possible to detect the formation of a dual information system, similar to the one noted earlier for telecommunications, in which the poor will be priced out of the markets for new television-based services and left with a structure of public provision that is increasingly unable or unwilling to deliver the range of general information required for full citizenship.

Conclusion

The developments outlined here raise a number of important issues for public policy, which deserve careful investigation and detailed debate. As a beginning, we need to break with the dominant view, fashionable across the political spectrum, that planning information provision is primarily a matter for policies directed at technology and industry, and to recognise that because adequate information is a basic precondition for real choice and effective political participation, ensuring its diversity and accessibility to all groups in society has to be a core concern of social and cultural policy.

References

1   Di Childs, Angela Hickey and Jane Winter, *Citizens' Advice: a study of who uses London's Citizens Advice Bureaux and the services they receive*, GLCAB, 1985, p 14.
2   J McKnight, 'Pressure points: the crisis in management', in S Ward (ed), *DHSS in crisis*, CPAG, 1985.
3   See Peter Golding and Graham Murdock, 'Unequal information: access and exclusion in the new communications marketplace', in Marjorie Ferguson (ed), *New Communication Technology and the Public Interest*, Sage Publications, 1986.
4   Karen McKay, Federation of Independent Advice Centres, letter to the *Guardian*, 10 February 1986.
5   *Employment Gazette*, December 1985, p 491.
6   Jack Summerscale and Chris Wells, *British Telecom*, De Zoete and Bevan, 1984, pp 121-46.
7   Steve Vines, 'BT's long distance bargains', *Observer*, 29 January 1984, p 28.
8   Quoted in Peter Large, 'BT warning of higher charges for private calls', *Guardian*, 15 October 1985, p 23.
9   Cabinet Office Information Technology Advisory Panel, *Making a Business of Information: a survey of new opportunities*, HMSO, September 1983, pp 27-35.
10 A S C Ehrenberg, 'What is the BBC worth?', *New Society*, 14 February 1985, pp 248-50.
11 Quoted in Stuart Smith, 'DER in satellite TV rental first', *Marketing Week*, 22 November 1985, p 11.
12 *Broadcast*, 31 January 1986, p 3.

CPAG's 21st ANNIVERSARY

For 21 years, we've kept up a steady flow of facts and figures about poverty, social security and related issues. Now, for our 21st, we want to do something special.

A Crunch Year for Welfare
A stark choice lies at the heart of the arguments about the future of Britain's Welfare State. Can we aim to prevent poverty — not just manage it?

A Fairer Future for Children
Someone once commented that you can judge society by how it treats its children. With nearly 4 million youngsters being brought up in poverty or its margins, Britain has plenty to be ashamed of.

Divided Britain
Virtually every aspect of our society reflects divisions based on income, power, wealth, race and sex. That's why we've decided to mount a nationwide series of events aimed at bringing home the scale of the problems and what can be done to change things for the better.

We are working closely with local groups, councils, churches, trade unions and others, culminating in an impressive week of activities from 28 June to 6 July 1986.

Join in CPAG's 21st Anniversary Year
☐ Yes, I would like to support this work with a donation of £ _____
☐ Yes, I would like to join as a Comprehensive Member (£25/year), and be sent all CPAG's major pamphlets, rights books, bulletin and journal.
☐ Yes, I would like to be sent details of other membership options.
☐ Yes, I am willing to support CPAG by making a covenant.

I enclose a cheque/PO for £ _____ (payable to CPAG)

Name _____

Organisation (if any) _____

Address _____

_____

Town _____

County _____ Postcode _____

Please send details about ☐publications ☐branches ☐affiliations
Send to: **CPAG, 1 Macklin Street, London WC2B 5NH**